Tennis Instruction for Fun and Competition

Tennis Instruction for Fun and Competition

Virginia Kraft

Photographs by William B. Kegg III
except where otherwise noted

Publishers · GROSSET & DUNLAP · New York
A FILMWAYS COMPANY

To Erza and George Hartman, who have demonstrated to several generations of Gipsy Trailers that tennis is a game of champions.

The author wishes to thank Patricia Robinson, Marian Taylor and George Kandle, the three principal photographic subjects in this book, for their patience, cooperation and good humor. Thanks too are due to Judy Barta, Donna and Gordon Fales, Joseph Grandlienard, Erza and George Hartman, Felice and Alfred Meyer, Gilbert Robinson and many fellow Gipsy Trailers for their help, encouragement and support.

Portions of Part I originally appeared in an article by the author in the Summer 1972 issue of *Eastern Tennis*. Copyright © 1972 by Eastern Tennis. The Official Rules of Lawn Tennis are reprinted by permission from *The Official USLTA Tennis Yearbook*. Copyright 1974 by United States Lawn Tennis Association.

Contents

Preface 7
PART I: MY STORY
   I "Nobody Learns to Play Tennis in One Season" 9
  II The Experiment Begins 14
 III Strange Partners 18
 IV Tennis Elbow and Other Ailments 25
  V Back Home at Gipsy Trail 30
 VI The Tournament Opens 39
VII End of the Experiment 45

PART II: INSTRUCTION
VIII Balance and Grip 48
 IX The Forehand and Backhand 63
  X The Drop-shot, Half-volley and Lob 92
 XI The Volley 97
XII The Serve 107
XIII The Overhead Smash and Return of Serve 121
XIV Strategy 127

PART III: ETIQUETTE AND RULES
 XV Courtsmanship 136
XVI The Rules of Lawn Tennis 149

GLOSSARY 165
INDEX 175

Preface

Wherever I go these days, I pack a tennis racket and when I get there, I use it. Nothing has ever proved a better way to make friends or a greater source of entertainment and pleasure. I have played with rank beginners, with tournament stars, with people who spoke no English, with small children, with elderly men, with the owner of a famous hotel, with the beautician at that hotel, with a French chef, an Australian executive, an Eskimo photographer, and with many, many other interesting partners. Most I would never have met except for my tennis racket. Many were much better players than I. Some were worse. But we all had one wonderful interest in common: tennis. It is the game for all seasons, all places, all people.

I am proof of this. I came to tennis as an adult, with poor coordination and no natural talent but with eagerness to learn and enthusiasm for the sport. My efforts, discouraging at times, have been rewarded a thousandfold by the pleasures the game has brought me. I shall never appear on the center court at Wimbleton or Forest Hills, or on almost any other center court for that matter, but I am a tennis player and I hope to enjoy the game to the end of my days. This is an account of how I became a tennis player and some things I learned along the way.

PART I: My Story

I. "Nobody Learns to Play Tennis in One Season"

For thirteen years I lived within 100 yards of the tennis courts at Gipsy Trail Club in Carmel, New York. For thirteen years, from the last snowfall in March to the first flurries in November, I awakened each morning to the *whup whup whup* of tennis balls being hit by my energetic neighbors. And for thirteen years I tried to shut the whole ridiculous game out of my sleep and my life. Alas, I could do neither.

For one thing I was married to a tennis nut at the time. He did not carry his racket to the altar but it came along on the honeymoon and was seldom out of his hands thereafter. If his defection to the courts on every weekend, holiday and spare afternoon was not clue enough that *his* love was bigger than *ours,* the mountains of sweaty, soggy laundry it produced made the fact oppressively clear.

But of all the annoyances, the one which really got to me during those thirteen years I spent on the outside of the "in" sport at our house was the way the subject continuously intruded upon conversation. It was one thing to listen to balls being hit all day. It was another to listen to *how* they were hit all

evening. Neither war nor weather nor the latest Wall Street whim had a conversational chance once someone began dissecting the play. In our set, love always carried a number. The hottest gossip was never who was sleeping with whom but who was playing mixed doubles with whom.

For a time I tried acting as if I understood what everyone was talking about. But the truth is, I never did. The language of tennis, unlike the language of love (the emotion, that is), is undecipherable without the code. And in those days at Gipsy Trail, no tennis player was going to let an outsider in on the code.

The final frustration came when my children took up with the enemy. Dozens of *little* white shorts and shirts began appearing among the big ones on wash days. Closets grew ankle-deep in sneakers of assorted sizes. Rackets, balls and empty cans were constant reminders of the foreign world that lay just 100 yards beyond my door. It was too much. After thirteen years, I rebelled.

"I have decided to take up tennis," I announced one spring evening to my husband. "At least maybe then I'll see

9

you once in a while. We'll be able to play together, and maybe we can even enter the Mixed Doubles this year."

Had I told him that the children had flunked, the bank had foreclosed, the market had failed and the baby-sitter had quit—all in one day—he could not have looked more startled. After a long and ominous pause, during which he stared at me as if I were some mysterious insect that had suddenly appeared in his martini, he said in a strangely controlled voice: "I have decided to take up concert piano." There was another pause. "It might be fun to play at Carnegie next month."

Then he exploded.

"Mixed doubles! Are you out of your mind? You are speaking of *tennis*. TENNIS! Not skiing. Not sailing. Not *sled-dog racing*." There was a sneer to this last. The year before I had indeed tackled the sport of sled-dog racing and many bruised and battered extremities later had guided my heroic dog team, which deserved 100 percent of the credit, to a respectable sixteenth-place finish in the World Sled-dog Racing Championships in Anchorage, Alaska.

"Do you honestly believe," Bob went on, "that you can simply go out and *take up* tennis? Just like that! A few lessons and off to the tournaments. Hah! To begin with, you are twenty-five years too late!" He had his racket now and he smashed at an imaginary overhead for emphasis.

"This is a game you start as a child," he said in a tone clearly reserved for children. Naughty children. "And you spend the rest of your life learning. Even then, a lot of people never master tennis. Billie Jean Kings are in short supply these days."

"Wimbledon and Forest Hills were

not on my schedule," I said, stunned by the reaction my innocent proposal had evoked. "I simply want to learn the play the game well enough to play here at the club, the way the rest of you play, for fun. If I am going to take the trouble to learn the game, I might just as well plan on entering the tournaments Labor Day weekend. Everybody else here does, so why not?"

"Why not fly?" Bob shouted, swinging his racket. "Nobody learns to play tennis in one season, and I mean *nobody*. As for learning to play well enough even for our tournaments, which are certainly not Wimbledon, if you started this minute and practiced every day for the next ten years, you would be lucky to make them."

It was an interesting challenge. But Bob's attitude, I discovered, was not unique. It was shared, I learned with great surprise, by most of the people to whom I mentioned the idea, including nontennis players.

"You can take up skiing or riding and learn enough in a season to at least have fun with the sport," a nontennis-playing friend told me in explaining why she did not play. "But with tennis, you spend years taking lessons before you even reach the stage where someone will hit a ball with you. At our age, who has the time?"

It was a good question, and most of the evidence suggested she was right. Unfortunately, as late as the end of the 1960s, the myth that tennis must be embraced first in childhood, that it must be nurtured over countless years of trial and training, that it accepts no late-bloomers and permits no unconventional courtships, had been so firmly established in most clubs such as mine that few nonplaying adults dared set foot on a court. The odd, courageous soul who did—and it took courage, believe me—was so thoroughly intimidated, humiliated or ignored that once was usually more than enough.

The boom that has in a few brief years made tennis the fastest-growing sport in America had not yet begun. Tennis was still the exclusive property of the select, and it was not about to be opened up to the masses. Not if the old guard had its way. This negative attitude towards newcomers, which I had not encountered seriously before because I had not seriously considered taking up the sport before, was appalling. It was, in fact, downright un-American. It made no sense that I, and countless others like me, should be closed out forever from the sport that is perhaps played in more parts of the world than any other game, purely and simply because someone failed to put a racket in our hands at age ten. Why should participation in this singularly lifetime sport be determined by the whims of one's fifth-grade physical education teacher? And why should those who already played and loved tennis be so unwilling to accept newcomers arriving at the game late or by routes other than the well-traveled ones? There were reasons, I suppose, but I never did discover them.

The more I thought about the sport and the shibboleths that had made it a closed society for so long, the more shortchanged I began to feel. So I *was* over thirty, and a little overweight, and not very athletically endowed and not too well coordinated either. So I had never (for reasons I could not even remember, but they probably had something to do with growing up in New York City) played tennis as a child or

even as a teen-ager. Were these sufficient causes to banish me to the sidelines forever? I didn't think so. I decided the time had come not only to take up tennis, but also to take it on. Before going any further, let me make it perfectly clear that I had no fantasies about changing my name from Kraft to King. I had long ago decided that the world needed Shirley Booths as well as Marilyn Monroes, and so far as this philosophy applied to sports (not to mention quite a few other areas), I definitely belonged in the former, not the latter, category.

The level of tennis I aspired to was modest. I wanted to learn the game well enough to go out on a court and not feel like an idiot, or worse, a leper. In other words, I wanted to acquire enough skill, knowledge and confidence to play average club-level tennis without embarrassment, apology or catastrophe. Most of all, I wanted to feel enough at ease with the game to enjoy it.

I had, of course, another small objective, which must be confessed. After all the big talk by all the old guard about the sanctity of the sport, there was something delicious in the possibility of proving them wrong. My goal, after all, was not an extraordinary one. Besides, it seemed to me that if I could learn the game well enough in one season to play on a socially acceptable club level, this would certainly prove that the sport was within the reach of many more people than were currently enjoying it. Better still, if I could master it enough to make even a modest showing in the Labor Day tournaments, a lot of old "truths" would be shattered.

The idea was totally intriguing. It was also totally impossible to implement at Gipsy Trail Club. My sled dogs would have had a better chance on those courts than I. The answer was to learn the game somewhere else and then to return, triumphant, in time for the tournaments. Except on this venture, I would not have the dog team to help me. This was strictly a solo.

The idea proved equally intriguing to Richard W. Johnston, who was then Assistant Managing Editor of *Sports Illustrated,* and a man endowed with ample quantities of both imagination and humor. In my years as a writer for the magazine, he had gone along with a number of zany proposals, including the sled-dog race, and so received this one with open mind. We agreed that with my dubious athletic talents and less than a season in which to accomplish the goal, I would have to devote myself pretty completely to the project. I had no idea at the time just how completely that would be. I did know it meant time, courts and partners in almost unlimited quantities. This in turn meant the unhappy prospect of being away from home for several weeks. It also meant the best available instruction.

After numerous conferences with various members of the magazine's tennis department, all of whom shared in assorted degrees our enthusiasm for the proposed experiment, Welby Van Horn was selected as the best possible instructor for the task ahead. Few teaching professionals in any sport could boast the record of success he enjoyed. A list of his protégés reads like a *Who's Who* of Tennis, with 134 national rankings among them, including 1967's top-ranked United States Player Charles Pasarell. Once a precocious World Class player, Van Horn was one of the youngest finalists ever to play at For-

est Hills when, at nineteen, he lost the 1939 Championship to the indomitable Bobby Riggs, then in his prime. Van Horn turned professional two years later, and now had more than a quarter-century of teaching experience. The credentials were impressive.

There was one snag. (There always is.) Welby's chief interest at that time was in young players. Very young, like ten, eleven and twelve years old. When he did bother to teach adults, which was as seldom as possible, he made little effort to disguise his disinterest. But Welby, too, was intrigued by the idea. The more arguments he raised against it, and he raised plenty of them, the more challenging the possibilities became to him.

My good fortune in snaring Welby was offset by the fact that the instruction would have to take place in San Juan, Puerto Rico, where Welby was pro at the Caribe Hilton Tennis Club. I had nothing personal against Puerto Rico. In spring, fall and winter it is a grand and glorious vacation land. But in summer it is just plain hot, and summer, alas, was the season we were talking about.

There were four doubles courts at the Caribe Hilton, surfaced in Cork-Turf and set two-by-two at right angles to the beach and ocean. At night they were lighted electrically and cooled by tropical breezes. By day, in summer at least, the temperatures were at the baking level and everybody in his right mind retreated to the beaches. Everybody, that is, except me and a bunch of Puerto Rican youngsters who discovered in my first days there that they had found at least one *yanqui* who was both *stupido* and *loco.* In those days, by their own industrious efforts, the children managed

Sports Illustrated photo by Frank Mullins. © Time Inc.

Welby Van Horn with star pupil, Freddy deJesus.

to cadge at least one out of every three balls per can that I exposed to the courts. Tennis now became not only a question of getting the ball over the net, but keeping it on the court. Whenever a ball rolled near a fence, a tiny brown hand from outside darted through

the mesh, moving as swiftly and surely as a barracuda, and gulped it down as decisively. Actually there was a back-up fence to guard against such occurrences, but rain or shine the children's appetite for tennis balls never seemed to abate, and I often wondered whether it was profit or pleasure that prompted such dedication.

Between half-hour lessons, which began as early as 8 and ran to dark, Welby answered the phone, assigned courts, lined up games for guests, strung rackets, replaced grips, dispensed towels, supervised the lockers and served as buyer, bookkeeper, merchandiser, stock clerk and salesman for the tennis gear and clothing he stocked.

He also mediated on- and off-court disputes, slowed down overeager athletes, soothed overanxious parents, settled teen-age tempests, placated the club's several prima donnas, disciplined its boisterous juniors and, when it rained (which was almost every day while I was there), personally swabbed off the courts with a king-size squeegee.

Except for two afternoons a week, when he played golf, and two weeks each fall, when he visited Forest Hills and relatives, this was Welby's life, seven days a week, fifty weeks of the year.

For five weeks that memorable summer, I added to the confusion.

II. The Experiment Begins

My departure from Gipsy Trail was veiled in cryptic allusions to a fishing story in the Caribbean that would tie me up for the first half of the summer. Nobody, fortunately, noted that fishing in the Caribbean is particularly poor in summer. And nobody suspected that I was off on a secret mission to infiltrate the club's sacred sport either.

I arrived in San Juan with three new tennis dresses, one pair of the latest synthetic tennis shoes, two pairs of tennis half-socks, a bad cold and, at Welby's recommendation, no racket. His choice from several dozen in his shop was a 14-ounce (light) Dunlop Maxply Fort racket with a 4½-inch grip, strung with nylon at 68-pounds tension. The only part of this I understood was that the racket was made of wood. Even I had heard about metal rackets, which had just come out, and I was a little disappointed not to be starting off with the latest in equipment. But Welby was adamant in his preference for wood and I was certainly in no position to argue.

Thus attired and equipped, the next step was to test my eye-hand coordination. Welby pushed a metal supermar- ket cart (one of his trademarks, I soon learned) filled with used tennis balls out on his teaching court and stationed me in the center of the service court on one side of the net. He stood on the base line opposite. I fingered my racket admiringly, flexing in the new tennis shoes and feeling exactly like someone straight out of a Salem cigarette ad.

"Hold the racket any way it is comfortable to you," Welby said. "When I throw the ball, try to hit it back at me with the racket."

He threw. I swung. The ball bounced somewhere behind me.

"Don't look at me, look at the ball," he said.

Again he threw. Again the ball bounced behind me.

"Forget the racket. Concentrate on the ball."

I tried again. This time I hit the ball squarely and it bounded off the strings of my Dunlop back towards him. I was elated.

"That's it," he said. "Watch the ball."

That message was to haunt me in the days ahead. And as easy as watching the ball may sound, it proved, at

least for me, to be unbelievably difficult. Somehow just as the ball and
racket met, I invariably looked elsewhere. It was an unconscious, almost a
reflex action. It was not by any means
to be my only problem.

By the end of the first week we had
determined beyond any doubt that my
reflexes were slow (age?), that my timing was poor, that my ability to anticipate the ball was sadly deficient and
that I had absolutely no ball-sense. (I
had not even known there was such a
thing.) In fact, by the end of the first
couple of days it was all too clear that
I was about the worst athletic prospect
Welby had ever encountered.

"Didn't you ever play any kind of
ball?" he asked incredulously. "Catch?
Ping-Pong? Anything?"

The answer, alas, was no. There had
been no boys in my family. I had
grown up in a city apartment, and in
school I had managed by devious and
clever methods to evade physical education classes where I might have been
exposed to at least a few of the ball
sports. I was paying for it now, and
Welby had no intention of letting me
off cheaply.

He seemed to take perverse pleasure
in tossing balls at me when I least expected them. His expression as I fumbled with both hands to catch them, often in my skirt, was a combination of
disgust, disbelief and pity. Any hope
that I might prove to be a natural tennis player vanished the first week. There
was even serious doubt I could be an
unnatural player! Welby spent most of
that first disillusioning week acquaint-
ing me with what he outlined as the
four basic fundamentals of tennis: balance, grip, stroke and strategy, in that
order.

"The only *strategy* you need worry
about as a beginner," he said, "is getting the ball back over the net. To do
that, you must *stroke* it. To stroke it
properly, you must have the proper
grip. And to do any of these things,
your feet and your body must be in
proper position and *balance*. So, logically, before you can do anything with
the ball, you must learn balance."

To demonstrate the proper body position and footwork, Welby stood with
me before the darkened windows of the
trophy room, which reflected our im-
ages as clearly as if they were mirrors.
Welby stood sideways to the mirror and
went through the motions of a forehand
drive, meeting an imaginary ball with
an imaginary racket at right angles to
the mirror, then following through so
that he completed the imaginary stroke
with his body facing the mirror, his
weight on the ball of his left (or anchor) foot and his right hand on about
a line with his left ear. The motion was
as smooth and graceful as a ballet step.
I imitated his movements, getting the
feeling of rotating my body, shifting
my weight to my anchor foot and following through in the slightly exaggerated manner that was another distinctive Welby trademark.

For hours I stood before those darkened windows, repeating the motions
over and over again while Welby at-
tended to his other pupils and chores.
To the casual passerby, I must have
looked totally demented.

At night I practiced the same motions before the mirror in my hotel
room, sometimes balancing a book on my
head to make certain that head, hips
and heels were all in the right place at
the right time.

Then to improve my poor eye and

poorer ball-sense, I bounced the ball on the floor with my racket a few thousand times, keeping the racket at hip level and trying to keep the ball on the center of the strings. It was a fatiguing and maddening exercise. My arm and wrist ached after the first hundred bounces and the task became a contest with myself to see how long I could last.

It was a fascinating way to spend an evening in San Juan. Nobody would have believed that either. Sometimes, even I did not.

On the third day we worked on proper forehand and backhand grips, which should have been easy, but like everything else about the sport, were a problem for me. The backhand went okay, but the forehand (Welby taught a standard Eastern grip) defied me.

"The racket is not a club," Welby said. "Think of it as a musical instrument, a violin." I thought of it as a violin but I gripped it as if it were a tuba trying to get away. At least my sessions before the mirror were now *with* a racket which, while hard on the lamps in my room, made me somewhat less conspicuous when practicing on the courts.

The next step was to hit balls. Initially Welby threw them to me, as he had that first day. Only now I knew what it was all about. But knowing, I soon learned, was not doing. Welby placed four balls on the ground to delineate the strike zone—the area in which racket and ball actually meet. As the ball he tossed approached the strike zone, I went through the motions I had been practicing so diligently all week. Pivot. Stroke. Follow through.

The form was perfect. The only problem was that I missed the ball. We tried again. And again. Sometimes I stroked too soon. Sometimes not soon enough. When I did hit the ball, it was rarely with the center of the strings but with the racket frame or throat or, now and then, the middle of the handle—which is not easy to do.

"Watch the ball, watch the ball," Welby chanted. He changed tactics. Instead of bouncing the ball to me, he had me drop the ball myself and then hit it on the bounce. My hit average increased from 10 percent to 11 percent. We both agreed that I was not watching the ball at the critical moment but neither of us could figure out how to make me do so.

"Instead of bouncing the ball, try hitting it out of your hand," Welby suggested. "Don't let it bounce at all."

This helped. From then on, whenever I started the ball, I did it this way. But it was not until the second week that we stumbled upon the trick which forced me, finally, to keep my eyes on the ball.

I was rallying, and I use the word about as loosely as it can be used, with one of Welby's protégés, Ramón "Chollo" Almonte, who was also serving as assistant pro that summer. Chollo was twenty, in college and wholly sympathetic to my plight. But he seemed as mystified as Welby and I about how to solve it. Although my average had improved so I was hitting about 70 percent of the balls he placed to me, at least 50 percent of those were miss-hits. My racket by now looked antique and abused, and I was beginning to look the same.

As afternoon turned to evening, the courts grew dark. Instead of turning on the floodlights, Chollo continued to hit balls to me. Suddenly in the almost total darkness, I discovered that I was hitting the balls and returning them better than I ever had before. The poor visibility had apparently forced from me that extra measure of concentration necessary to keep my eyes on the ball throughout the stroke. For the first time I was actually able to see the ball leaving the strings of my racket. Why this should have carried over to daylight remains a mystery, but from that point on, I had won at least one of the battles.

III. Strange Partners

As I began to feel I knew what I was doing, and that at last I was doing it properly, even the oppressive heat of the Puerto Rican summer could not keep me off the courts. The sense of accomplishment was exhilarating. Everything seemed to be falling into place. My strokes were visibly improving each day, and my rhythm and timing, both of which left much to be desired, were at least recognizable. With reasonable regularity I was hitting balls that not only sounded good but also occasionally made it to the opposite base line—of the court I was playing on!

If I was not taking a lesson from Welby, and his supermarket basket of tennis balls was free, I practiced my struggling serve for as long as I could bear the frustration of that exercise. This was seldom for more than two, at the most three, baskets of balls. By then I had managed to crack the racket across my shinbone enough times on the follow-

through to turn my legs purple, and my language even more so. The serve is considered by many professionals to be the most difficult part of the game to teach and the hardest for a beginner to learn. Putting everything together requires so much coordination and timing. During my entire stay in Puerto Rico I never did get everything together where the serve was concerned. I think Welby decided that it was hopeless, and so devoted his efforts with me to other aspects of play.

My attempts at the backboard were equally hopeless. Certainly to most tennis players, there is no training exercise of as much value as the backboard. The late Midwestern coach Jean Hoxie was almost fanatical when it came to making her students work out on it. Many pros, such as Peaches Bartkowicz, who could hit 950 volleys off a backboard during a single session without bouncing the ball on the ground once, attribute much of their tournament success to such training.

But most of Jean Hoxie's protégés were athletically gifted young people with the skill and reflexes necessary for that kind of exercise. I was not. Even under ideal conditions, I would have found a backboard beyond my abilities at that stage. The ball comes off a backboard too fast for most neophytes, demanding quicker reflexes and more precise timing than they usually have.

The backboard setup at the Caribe Hilton magnified this problem for me. It was rectangular and about half as wide as a regular tennis court. Its side fences were a stone wall on the left, which separated it from a busy San Juan thoroughfare and a McDonald's eatery, and the fence of the last regular tennis court on the right, through which one entered.

The backboard itself was the rear end of a one-story cinder-block building that was used as the gardener's greenhouse and tool shed. A white line representing the net had been painted across this building. The concrete playing surface extended from there, barely beyond what would be the service line on a regular court, ruling out groundstroke returns, which, in turn, meant losing out on an important element of practice. Beyond it was a small tropical jungle of trees and plants interspersed with large coral-like outcroppings.

Since a majority of my balls bounded off the wall and over my shoulder before I could get my racket even vaguely close to them, I spent a lot of time in that garden spot. Those balls which did not wind up in the jungle came to rest at the feet of McDonald's patrons outside or in a dark six-inch corridor between the stone wall and the green-house, and thus were lost forever. The attrition rate of balls and the utter frustration of the backboard experience made some other form of solo practice essential.

The most enjoyable and rewarding was working out with the Moody Trainer. This was a rather odd and wondrous piece of equipment, so simple it might have been made by a child but so useful and versatile that it had clearly been invented by a genius. It consisted of an ordinary tennis ball threaded with a stout string which was attached to a long, heavy-duty rubber band. The other end of the rubber band was fastened into a small sand-filled bag which served as a ground weight.

The Moody Trainer was best on an actual tennis court, but it could be used on any flat surface about a half-court in length. The trainer was set up on the service line, and the ball was started by hand from a point almost to the base line behind the bag, then hit —either forehand or backhand—over the net. If the stroke was good, the ball touched ground on the other side, bounded back over the net, bounced again in about center court and presented itself for another forehand or backhand. This could be varied by moving in closer to the net and volleying the ball on the return.

In a sense, the Moody Trainer was a grown-up version of the little rubber ball on an elastic that children bounce off a wooden paddle by the hour to entertain themselves. It did more than entertain me. At that stage it was by far the most useful training exercise I could undertake alone. The Moody Trainer was an obliging and always faithful partner. It was also the only one available in those early days.

Not that there was a shortage of people on the courts. There were plenty of regulars at all times, particularly in late afternoons and evenings when the heat of the scorching sun had abated and a slight breeze blew in off the water. These were mainly business people from San Juan and vicinity who came in twosomes or foursomes and seldom mixed outside their specific groups. During the day there was always a sprinkling of tourists from the hotel and a mob of teen-agers. But these were not ordinary teen-agers, nor was the tennis they played ordinary. Most were protégés of Welby's who, in addition to brushing up their games between the end of school and the beginning of the Junior Nationals, also made the tennis club their social hangout.

They were beautiful to watch on the courts but somewhat formidable to encounter in a group. Then they giggled, joked, jabbered away in Spanish and barely acknowledged anyone or anything except Welby's periodic reprimands. They also clearly mistrusted anyone over thirty, especially someone from New York who took so many lessons and made so little progress. My hesitant *"Buenos días"* invariably evoked gales of laughter but seldom a return greeting. The adult regulars, including a number of the teen-agers' parents, were slightly less unapproachable. They at least returned my greeting.

The only human being, in fact, who made any friendly overture at all in the first ten days was a florid-faced, paunchy German who not only opened the conversation on several occasions but even volunteered appropriately guttural words of encouragement about my tennis. He was, it turned out, a land salesman who thought he had spotted a rich mark. When he discovered his mistake he returned to prospecting more productive fields in the Hilton lobby and was never seen on the courts again.

And then I met A. Marvin Wohlmutter. I arrived at Welby's pro shop as usual one morning at 8 to find the shutters down and the door locked. Welby, it later turned out, had run into some domestic problem and for the first time in months failed to show up at the appointed hour to perform his daily rituals. Since locked inside his shop was my Moody Trainer and all the balls, this left me at loose ends. I was pondering my next move when a miniature figure in white appeared at my elbow. He was just over four feet tall and consisted almost entirely of angles and protruding joints. On his beaklike nose was perched an enormous pair of horn-rimmed glasses with the thickest lenses I have ever seen. He carried a tennis racket and an unopened can of balls. I eyed the balls covetously.

"Buenos días," I said in my friendliest fashion.

"I speak English," he replied, very seriously. He extended a hand to shake. "A. Marvin Wohlmutter is the name. New Canaan, Connecticut. Beautiful setting here, although I really prefer clay. Tennis is a more artistic game on clay, don't you agree?"

"Um," I mumbled, trying to decide if he was a midget or a child. He looked somewhere between ten and twelve years old. He acted forty.

"Do you play here much?" I asked.

"Not regularly," he said. "My grandparents live nearby. I spend two weeks with them every summer. It is an excellent opportunity to hone my game. Van Horn is one of the best, you know." I nodded knowingly. "Since he seems to be nowhere in sight," he added, "would you care to hit a few?"

The words were magic. No one had ever said them to me before. Poor A. Marvin Wohlmutter, I thought, watching him open the can of balls and stride purposefully onto the court. Little do you know that you are about to become my first *human* partner. I was actually going "to hit a few." With a real, live person. The thought was intoxicating.

The play, if it could be called that, was the ultimate test of A. Marvin Wohlmutter's twelve-year-old poise. He came through with flying colors. Considering what he was up against, this is a genuine tribute to A. Marvin.

He started out under the impression that he faced across the net another *player*. Even a seasoned player fumbles a shot or two warming up. But every shot? Perhaps it was the overwhelming pressure of a flesh-and-blood partner at last, or perhaps just an off morning, but whatever the cause, I went into a state of total regression. All those baseline shots were gone. All those fine Moody forehands deserted me. I floundered hopelessly after A. Marvin's drives, never quite catching up to them, looking to all the world like an elephant trying to toe-dance.

And that marvelous, stoic little old man in a boy's body bore with it to the bitter end. He even thanked me when it was over. If ever anyone deserved the Medal of Honor, it was A. Marvin Wohlmutter, Gentleman. A. Marvin, God bless him, was the first of an influx of annual summer members who began arriving at the club in the next few weeks. The ladies' locker was suddenly transformed from a teen-age lair to the strategy center of San Juan's transient jet set. Each day, fresh from beauty parlors and boutiques, the chic, carefully lacquered Mainland wives showed up at the club for a round of tennis,

daiquiris and lunch on the terrace, and a sampling of the latest Island gossip.

Since half the American women did not speak to the other half, and since I was available and in evidence at almost any time of day, my social stature took a decided change for the better. Somebody always needed a fourth, and under the circumstances, they could not afford to be choosy. But unlike the teenagers, these ladies, or at least the ones who bothered to play with me, did nothing for Welby's image.

"Ninety-five percent of the tennis population plays tennis," he told me, "but only five percent are tennis players." It was soon clear what he meant. Except for their experience in procedure and scoring, which I needed, none of the American women I played with did much to improve my game. But they did give me an initial glimpse into ladies' tennis and it was almost enough to make me give up the sport.

My maiden venture onto the courts in bona fide play was ladies' doubles. It was a memorable introduction to the game. The ladies first debated which court had the least wind and the most shade, then who would play with whom, then who would play what side, then who would serve first. Each question involved considerable argument. Nobody agreed on anything. There then followed heated discussion about how many "free serves" were permitted before the ball finally landed in the proper court. Although none of the books mention it, I soon learned "first one in" is a hallmark of ladies' tennis.

After her tenth abortive effort into the net, the gal who provoked this discussion switched to serving underhanded and managed to dribble a ball into my service court. As I started forward to return it, my partner hit me with a flying tackle that almost knocked me down. Remarkably, she also returned the serve. This was not easy, considering how far she had had to travel. Unfortunately the ball went out so we lost the point, but one way or another, we made most of the others.

My partner, I discovered, was not one to be defeated easily, nor was she above helping her own cause even if this involved some liberties with the rules. After one really flagrant violation, I asked timidly if her shot had been legal.

"Of course not," she said, looking at me as if I were an idiot. "But that's their problem. If they don't call it, it's their tough luck."

She was, I noticed, very particular about calling any real or imagined violations on our opponents' part. She also kept the loudest score, and hers seemed to be the only one that counted, regardless of what the others thought. The opposition finally grew so disgruntled, and the arguments so distracting, that Welby stepped in as referee. His presence immediately demoralized all three ladies. For some odd reason, he had exactly the opposite effect on me. I suddenly played better. We won the set. We could even have won it legally. It was the first time I had seen Welby smile. In fact, he laughed out loud.

Singles proved less contentious but equally exasperating. My first opponent was a chubbyish redhead who played what might most charitably be described as a hopeless game. Her form was the antithesis of everything Welby taught. Her strokes were more like swats, and she swung her racket as if it were a baseball bat. We started off hitting a few, or trying to. Red definitely came off second best. It was too good to be true. The more she flubbed and fumbled balls, the better I looked. At last,

I thought, I have finally found a player worse than I. It was a wonderful sensation. It was also short-lived.

Whatever Red lacked in form seemed not to matter in play. The score after two sets was 0–6, 0–6. She clobbered me, but good.

Where were all those deep drives I had been hitting with Welby and Chollo? What had happened to the backhand that was beginning to look promising in practice? What of the form, the strokes, the follow-through I had so meticulously practiced? What happened was simple. I never had an opportunity to use anything I had learned.

Red plinked little, ineffectual shots to me, dribbling balls over the net so that they barely cleared the tape. Welby had drilled me to stand behind the base line to receive service. With Welby serving, this was the place to be. With Red serving, it put me at least 20 feet beyond her version of an ace.

By the middle of the second set I had adjusted to the fact that Red's strongest drive came over the net with the speed of a defrocked badminton bird. But even this newfound wisdom was of little use. I could no more sprint from the base line to the net fast enough to return one of her balls than I could predict to which side of the court it would be directed. It is only fair to note that Red had no better idea than I of where her balls were going. This lent a sort of mystery to the game. It also demoralized me.

"Now you know why it is a handicap to play with poor players," Welby told me after the fiasco. "They don't know what they are doing, and soon neither do you. It can ruin your game and your confidence."

Since I had neither a game nor confidence at that stage, I assumed I had little to lose, but Welby's comment shed some light on why experienced players are often reluctant to play with beginners, and clarified one of the enigmas of tennis.

"Playing with someone who is better than you are," Welby said, "is one of the best ways to improve your game. The problem is that everybody wants to play with somebody better, and nobody wants to play with a beginner. If the beginner is lucky, he winds up finding somebody who is progressing at his own level and they grope along together. If he is not, he winds up with the perpetual duffers, the duds who never learn or try to learn, and they usually do his game more harm than good.

"So be choosy," he added. "Play only with good players."

Welby's advice made sense in theory, but from a practical point of view, it seemed to have some holes. How, for example, does one find a partner who is superior if that partner is also looking for a partner who is superior? Somebody sooner or later is going to have to play beneath his level. If playing with a partner better than oneself is so valuable, why would anybody consent to play with a partner who is worse? What happens when none of the better players is willing to play with a beginner?

Every beginner, I discovered as the summer progressed, discovers for himself the answer to the last question. When none of the better players is willing to play with him, he simply is not included in their games. He can sit on the sidelines all day, day after day, even when a foursome is reduced to three and resorts to Canadian Doubles, and still not be asked to fill in. Then he has two choices: he can go home, hurt, without ever having touched ball to racket, and the odds are that he never

will be asked to join that or any other foursome; or he can swallow his pride and improve his game by working out on the Moody Trainer or the backboard. This is small compensation for actual play, especially for someone really desperate to get into a game, as I was many times in those early weeks, but it is sound advice. For an unskilled player in the first stages of tennis, either of these practices is many times better than playing with someone of lesser skill.

As for good players willingly playing beneath themselves, many do so occasionally, or regularly, for a variety of reasons. The most obvious is necessity. Partners cannot be programmed on a computer. There is always someone at the top of the tennis ladder and someone at the bottom, with most of the players in between. Even if those at or near the top play only with each other, there are bound to be differences among them, which will pair a good player with someone of lesser, or greater, skill. This is not only inevitable but healthy.

Beyond necessity, there is common courtesy, although this has certainly been abused in many clubs, surprisingly often by people who would not tolerate impoliteness under other circumstances. Fortunately the boom in tennis is changing this. There are more and more good players today, and happily the number who care enough to help a beginner is growing. They recognize that more competition produces better tennis for everyone.

Although a beginner cannot afford to play beneath himself in the early stages, a good player can do so without damaging his own game. A strong, consistent player who can place the ball exactly where he wants it can contribute immeasurably to a neophyte's progress, psychologically as well as physically.

Just as a bad player can make a good player look bad, a good player can make a bad player look good. Welby's and Chollo's balls were many times easier for me to return than Red's could ever be. The chance to play, if only a game or two, with a superior partner is a genuine boost to anybody's morale. Those who take up the game late in life are much more aware of this than those who cannot remember when they were beginners. As one who remembers vividly, the games of that summer stand out as peaks along a course that had more than its share of depressions.

IV. Tennis Elbow and Other Ailments

As my game progressed, my physical condition deteriorated. Slowly but surely I began falling apart. The tropical sun, aided by the antibiotics I had taken the first week for my strep throat and cold, turned me a brilliant poppy color. My shoulders and forearms were raw. My feet were worse. I had eleven blisters, the largest of which made my big toe look as if it were encased in balloons. The surface temperature on the Caribe courts hit 100° F. at about 10 A.M. and continued on up through midday. In five weeks I literally melted through the soles of five pairs of tennis shoes, which had to be good for the tennis shoe business but very hard on my feet.

Then my right hand went. In addition to gaping blisters on palm, thumb and fingers, it became swollen and discolored. I began having trouble just holding on to the racket. Welby suggested that temporarily I use only my thumb and index finger, leaving the other fingers free. This helped. It forced me to relax the "death grip" I ordinarily put on the racket and thus eliminated much of the strain on my hand.

Next a pain like a toothache devel-oped in my right elbow. A similar ache appeared in my wrist. The two began signaling each other through my forearm. At first the arm hurt mainly when I hit balls. After a few days, the pain was there all the time.

I was waiting one afternoon for my lesson to begin, kneading my elbow as I did frequently, when a bald man with a big black mustache and a Groucho Marx leer came up to me and said: "Aha! I see you have it too." He could hardly contain his delight. On his right arm he wore a complicated series of straps and braces which straddled his elbow.

"Tennis elbow," he said knowingly, pointing first to his elbow and then to mine. "Worst thing that can happen to a tennis player."

"Oh, this is not tennis elbow," I told him. "I haven't been playing long enough for that. I understand tennis elbow comes from a calcium deposit that builds up in the joint over a period of time."

"Not true," he said, introducing himself as a doctor, a former tournament player and a self-proclaimed authority on tennis elbow. "Tennis elbow is a ten-donitis—an inflammation of the joint. It

25

can come on in a day. And it can take *years* to cure. That's what you've got. Spotted it right away."

We stood there rubbing elbows and comparing complaints as he expounded on what I was to learn was *the* occupational disease of the sport. I also learned after reading through some of the exhaustive literature on the subject that there are as many theories about what tennis elbow is as there are theories about how to cure it. One tennis-elbow authority broke them down as follows:

CAUSES	TREATMENT
Poor equipment	Better equipment
Strings too tight	Loosen strings
Strings too loose	Tighten strings
Grip too small	Enlarge grip
Grip too large	Reduce grip
Racket too heavy	Lighter racket
Racket too light	Heavier racket
Unnatural motion	Take lessons
Nylon strings	Gut strings
Gut strings	Nylon strings
No copper bracelet	Copper bracelet
Copper bracelet	No bracelet

On a more scientific plane, I discovered, *humeral epicondylitis,* as tennis elbow is known in the medical profession, is attributed to trauma, contusion, sprain, soft-tissue calcification, bursitis, *radiohumeral synovitis,* tear of the *tensor carpi radialis brevis* muscle, avulsion of the tendon origins, displacement of the orbicular ligament on the radial head and idiopathic spontaneous occurrence. In other words, take your choice.

Treatments include rest, massage, heat, a brace, whirlpool baths, ultrasound therapy, aspirin, hydrocortisone injections, roentgenotherapy and open-elbow surgery. The doctors, obviously, are as confused as the pros. A layman's

approach, I decided, might be as good as any. I wired home for a metal racket.

By the time it arrived, the pain in my elbow had grown so severe that I was unable to hit balls for more than a few minutes at a time. Each miss-hit jarred through my arm like a hammer blow. My performance went steadily downhill. At one point, exasperated, Welby said something about Pavlov and how he wished he could rig a device to give me an electric shock every time I miss-hit a ball. I did not have the strength to tell him that I would never measure up to Pavlov's dogs since the effect on my elbow of a miss-hit was far worse than any electric shock could be.

I did not have the courage, either, to tell him about the metal racket. I simply appeared on the court with it. By afternoon even Welby's obvious disapproval had softened. The effect of the new racket upon my elbow was dramatic. For the first time in more than a week I was able to hit through a two-hour session without flinching. The racket, a Sterling comparable in grip and weight to the Dunlop, seemed no different in feel and handling. But the difference in recoil was astonishing. Whereas with the wooden racket each poorly hit ball was transferred to my arm as a jarring shock, now I felt nothing at all. And as soon as I stopped anticipating pain, I began hitting the balls properly again. The recovery was remarkable.

Then the next disaster struck. I awoke one morning to find both my ankles swollen to twice their size. They looked as if tennis balls had been slipped under the skin. Somehow I managed to hide them from Welby and get through the morning's lesson, but my performance was miserable. Welby was disgusted.

"Run!" he jeered, as I tried to make my feet work. "Move!"

He began hitting balls first to one sideline, then to the other, so that I had to cross the width of the court for each shot. The harder I tried, the slower I became. The pain in my ankles grew worse. Perspiration ran from my arms onto my racket. The grip felt as if it were covered with oil. Finally the racket slipped out of my hand and bounced on the concrete. Welby turned on his heel and walked off the court with a scowl. I could not have lasted another minute.

By the next morning my ankles were completely discolored and the swelling was worse. It was impossible to hide them from Welby any longer.

"That's that," he said, shrugging his shoulders without looking up from the racket he was stringing. "If you can't run, you can't play."

"I can work on my strokes," I said. "I can work on my serve."

"Why don't you go home and come back next year?"

"You know I can't do that. The whole idea was to learn in one season. If I quit now, the experiment is a failure."

"So?" He shrugged. "Maybe it wasn't possible anyway."

"But you saw how I was playing two days ago. Everyone, including you, commented on how much I had learned." I was pleading now. I had worked too hard to give up in the middle. Besides, I had just tasted the first rewards of play, and had found that I loved the game.

"This is a setback, that's all," I insisted. "I am sure I'll be able to run in a few days. In the meantime, there is a lot I can work on without running."

Welby finished stringing the racket as if he had not heard me. I waited. Finally he ran his hand through his short-cropped hair and rubbed his eyes. Still not speaking, he uncapped a tube of zinc oxide and dabbed the white cream on the permanent burn marks on his nose, lips and forearms. Then he put the battered Welby hat on his head and reached under the counter for a towel. He thumbed through his collection of rackets on the wall and took down two. I watched him perform the various parts of his "going on the court" ritual, not daring to say a word. At last he backed the supermarket cart from behind a display case and rolled it towards the door.

"Okay," he said. "Let's get to work."

The next two weeks were a nightmare. Although I had asked a couple of tennis-playing doctors about them on the court one day, who told me the swelling would go away, my ankles showed little improvement and the pain was a constant, debilitating drain both physically and mentally. I could not believe that the game of tennis could so completely undo me. Nothing seemed to help my ankles. Welby's wife lent me a whirlpool foot bath. I tried cold water, hot water, Epsom salts, liniment, ice packs and heating pads. I consulted a physiotherapist but the pulling and twisting and kneading only compounded the pain. I tried keeping my feet up whenever I was not on court. When I was, I wrapped them in yards of Ace bandage. I ate aspirins as if they were candy, but they were of little help.

Neither was Welby. His sarcasm was unmerciful. This technique may be effective with children and teen-agers, but for me it was demoralizing. Day after day he chipped away at the shreds of my self-confidence. His criticisms were constant and demeaning. I seemed incapable of doing anything right. And the more he taunted me, the clumsier I became. I felt a complete fool. Finally the combination of Welby and my sore ankles was too much. I returned to my room one afternoon and broke down in tears. I hated myself. I hated tennis. And most of all, I hated Welby. If he was trying to break me, he was succeeding. Then, suddenly, I realized that was exactly what he *was* trying to do. He was testing me. And I was failing.

Now I was angry. Welby Van Horn was not going to run me off that court if I had to put my feet in casts and go out there on crutches! He was not going to defeat me. And neither was tennis. All at once, it was a new ball game.

It started off next morning like the old ball game. Welby was in rare form. I flubbed three of the first five balls and his sarcasm swelled.

"The-object-of-the-game," Welby sing-songed, "is-to-get-the-ball-over-the-net."

"That-is-what-I-am-trying-to-do, you-stupid-idiot," I sing-songed back under my breath. Think mean, I reminded myself. He's the villain. The system worked. I began hitting at least some of the balls the way I had before my ankles gave out. I felt meaner every minute.

Welby began another of his favorite torments: hitting balls back at me with the wrong hand, from behind his back and from between his legs. On one, he turned away as if to leave the court. I let the ball go by.

"You-have-to-hit-the-ball-to-get-it-over-the-net," he began in that maddening sing-song.

"I thought you were leaving the court," I said quite honestly. "I was afraid I might hit you."

This broke him up. "There is *no way* you could hit me," he sneered. "That takes skill." He hit another ball at me and then deliberately turned away.

"You asked for it, buddy-boy," I said

through clenched teeth. I hit the ball with everything I had. It left the strings of my racket like a missile, and it missed Welby's ear by a thousandth of an inch. He spun around, startled, and from the expression on his face it was clear that he, too, knew that this was a new ball game.

From then on, life was brighter. Even the teen-agers became friendly. I think they decided that anyone who would take on Welby and win—even so limited a victory—could not be all bad. They not only acknowledged and encouraged the improvement in my game but they also volunteered their time and considerable talents to play with me. After a steady diet of despair and disparagement from Welby, their sudden support was gloriously welcome. Afternoons, after my morning workouts with Welby and Chollo, I rallied with the teen-agers or took part in their informal doubles games. The advantage of playing with agile and expert thirteen-year-old partners was that they covered most of the court while I had only to worry about one little spot.

My ankles were improving but they were still a handicap. No matter how good my strokes became, they were useless if I could not get to the balls. Forcing myself to run did not work. The legs were willing but the ankles were not. I finally decided the best treatment might be a long weekend at home. But after four days of complete rest, my ankles were little improved. A visit to the local hospital proved why. To my dismay, I learned from X-rays and an orthopedic surgeon that I had an almost completely healed fracture of a small bone in my left ankle and a torn tendon in the right. (The tendon was slower to heal, which was why that ankle gave me more trouble.) Incredibly, on the day before I awoke to the nightmare of my distended ankles, I had somehow broken one, probably by stepping on a ball, and then doubtless in unconscious compensation for that injury, damaged the other.

"The break has healed remarkably well on its own," the doctor said, "but most people are aware of even a small one. If you had to do any walking on it, it must have been very painful." That was the understatement of the season.

The trip home, and the assurance that my ankles were mending, proved more than worth the loss of time. The hiatus was apparently as beneficial to Welby as to me. With only ten days of the experiment left, he showed definite signs of mellowing. The badgering and berating continued but occasionally he slipped and injected a kind word among the barbs. He seemed, at times, even genuinely pleased with my progress. Such approval, though tacit, after so much disapproval, was the ultimate spark to my morale. The last week was my best in Puerto Rico.

I spent most of it on the courts. Suddenly I had more partners than I could fit into the day. Almost everybody who had been at the courts in the previous weeks invited me to rally. With few exceptions, they were excellent tennis players, and they helped me compress at least a month's experience into that last week.

Throughout, Welby was never far away, nor was there much he missed. From another court his voice, like that of Big Brother, would remind me of a collapsed wrist or faulty footwork. As the week came to an end, he spent more and more time on the sidelines, saying little but watching thoughtfully. He seemed both amused and pleased at what he saw.

The last day in Puerto Rico was almost nostalgic. People stopped at the courts to say good-bye, others to exchange addresses, and Welby, in the manner of a principal at graduation exercises, made a little speech which was the closest he came to being loquacious.

"You may not think so now," he said, "but as you look back, you'll realize how far you came and how much you accomplished in a brief period. Don't expect to win games when you get home. You won't. Not for a while. But as a tennis player, your form and strokes and style are better right now than half the people who play *at* tennis. This is more important than scores.

"You have collected a good set of tools," Welby added. "Now take them home and put them to work."

I did not realize that this would be the hardest part of the experiment.

V. Back Home at Gipsy Trail

My entry into the tennis world at Gipsy Trail Club did not go unnoticed. Along with the intramural affairs and affronts of midsummer, it became one of the most actively discussed subjects of the season. One has to understand something about Gipsy Trail to appreciate why this was so.

Gipsy Trail is not a country club in the ordinary sense, nor is it a community; it is rather an entity, unique in many ways, that falls somewhere in between. It lies roughly 70 miles north of Times Square, midway between Peekskill on the Hudson River and Danbury in Connecticut, a hilly, woodsy, nature-lover's haven where whitetail deer still eat the rhododendrons, Canada geese nest on the shores of the lake and raccoons regularly outwit the residents by infiltrating their garbage bins after dark.

The club was started in the 1920s by a group of New York businessmen as a weekend retreat in what was then about as wild and virginal an area as any Manhattanite might sanely aspire to. First it consisted mainly of tents, but as the years passed, roads improved and New Yorkers became more intrepid. The tents grew to rough-hewn cabins,

and then kept on growing. Today they are still called cabins but the term, like much about Gipsy Trail, is habit. The club now consists of eighty "cabins," not one of which Abraham Lincoln, Henry Thoreau or Noah Webster could possibly identify with. It also encompasses within its still heavily wooded grounds an impressive fleet of Sunfish sailboats on its sailing and fishing lake; a trout pond; stables and many miles of riding trails; an excellent restaurant and bar; a lodge for nonresident members, of which there are a score or so in addition to the cabin-owning members; and five clay tennis courts—at least, that is what they are called.

Each year the tennis committee duly arranges for several tons of fresh clay to be spread on the courts, and each year the fresh clay duly washes off into the adjacent parking lots with the first torrential rains of spring. The drainage, alas, is almost as old as the club and so is somewhat constipated. But as with any venerable institution, change does not come easily to Gipsy Trail. In fact, it rarely comes at all. For three generations—and all three, in many cases, are alive and well and very much in residence—the chief reason for doing something at Gipsy Trail has been because it was always done that way.

Consequently when I arrived at the club as a new bride (having married rather than being born into the place which was a stigma in itself), I was relegated for then and for always to the ranks of the nonplayers. In the thirteen years I lived there before taking up the game, not only had I never set foot on the courts, which were after all only 100 yards from my back door, but I had not even watched a single game on them, or been invited to. With that kind of past, it was not surprising that my sudden appearance on the courts was regarded as bizarre behavior.

The inaugural event was simple enough. It was a Sunday afternoon, almost dark, when the courts, I hoped, would be deserted. I took a basket of balls and set up station on a rear court which was separated from the front ones by a plastic windscreen. After so many years, at last I stood on Gipsy Trail's most sacred soil. (Even I could tell that it certainly was not clay.) I served a few balls into the left court. Then I served a few into the right. I had a sense of moment about actually being there after so many years, no different, I am sure, from Chris Evert's at finding herself at last on the center court at Wimbledon. No one can spend any significant time at Gipsy Trail without being aware of the tradition that rubs off like mold.

Then, from behind the windscreen, there was a high-pitched squeal and the sound of a Boston-accented voice exclaiming: "Why, whoever can that be serving back there like that? I don't recognize the sneakers!"

Only minutes after my first brush with tradition I was found out. That is the way things are at Gipsy Trail.

I continued to serve. Concentration, Welby had drilled into me, is the key to tennis success.

"Why, it's Ginnie Kraft," the voice oozed through the windscreen. "Whatever are you doing on a tennis court? Girls, come look who is on the tennis court. Ginnie Kraft. Why, you don't even play tennis!"

Scratch the concentration. This was the moment of truth.

"Well, I was in Puerto Rico . . . on this fishing story, you see," I said lamely. Four faces peered at me through the windscreen as if I had just crawled out of a flying saucer and was still wearing my antennae. "There were these tennis courts there," I continued, "and sometimes when I wasn't fishing, you know, well . . . I took a few lessons." (I did not specify 60½ hours with Welby Van Horn and 32 with his assistant.) "I figured it might be fun to play, with the tennis courts so close to my house and all." I did not know what to say next.

The women continued to stare at me. I looked down self-consciously to see if anything was open that should not be. I realized afterwards, of course, that they were even more speechless than I. No one had ever decided, out of the blue, after thirteen years, that "it might be fun to play." One played or one did not. Changing the status quo at Gipsy Trail was simply not done.

Nor did anyone ever violate the pecking order of playing partners. Certain people played with certain people and certain other people did not. That was the way it was. When I, with no category at all, asked several of the best women players to hit with me, this was the ultimate breach of tradition.

"It's not done," exclaimed a friend in horror. "You can't just ask people like that to play with you. That is an insult!"

Insult or not, a number of the people I approached responded with enthusiasm. In fact, the most interesting fact that emerged from my unorthodox approach to partners was that there was an almost direct relationship between the amount of help offered to me and the skill level of those who offered it. The best players, with a few notable exceptions, were the most enthusiastic and generous with their help and time. Partly, of course, they could better afford to be than the poorer players, but it was more than that. These people had a genuine regard for the game which was reflected in their attitude that new faces on the courts could only be good for tennis at Gipsy Trail. It was the next skill level down, the intermediate players, who were the least receptive. Again, there were exceptions, but many seemed to view any newcomer on the courts as a vague, personal threat. This was a pattern that emerged early and remained fairly stable throughout the summer.

The Moody Trainer attracted almost as much attention on the courts the first week home as I did. For some unknown reason, since it is neither unique nor unavailable at most sports stores, nobody including Will Sherwood, the pro, had ever seen this type of training device before. It intrigued everybody.

Will was the club pro, but to maintain his amateur status as a college varsity player, he was officially hired as a counselor for the club's summer camp program. His camp duties involved about three hours of group tennis instruction four days a week. The rest of his time was available for private les-sons, which, in theory, were where he was supposed to make his folding money. His empty wallet attested to the inadequacies of the theory. Business, at least for the first half of the summer, had been miserable.

Will's immediate interest in the Moody Trainer was increased by the fact that I had gotten it from Welby Van Horn. Welby was one of Will's idols. On the junior circuit he had played against many of the Van Horn prodigies, including the younger Pasa-rells, and his knowledge of Welby's teaching techniques was surprisingly thorough. After our first conversation I decided to tell Will about the experiment. He was fascinated and eager to help.

Since most of Will's available time was still very much available, we mapped out a one-to-two-hour daily training program that would take me to the final tournaments on Labor Day weekend. Will made no attempt in these sessions to alter any of Welby's teachings. He worked instead on reinforcing and polishing what I had learned in Puerto Rico and on improving my speed and footwork. Both were serious problems. Will's efforts to solve them were heroic and imaginative.

He had me jogging around the courts, jumping rope, sprinting from base line to net and back, and doing all sorts of exercises. One of the most exhausting involved the use of two adjacent courts, which that first week we had no difficulty in finding empty. First I lobbed a ball to Will from one court. Then I dashed to the adjacent court, not taking my eyes from the ball, which Will returned in a high lob diagonally across the two courts. Will then dashed to the second court in time to receive my straight lob back, while I raced to the first court, hoping to arrive in time to receive his high diagonal lob across the two courts again. The object of sprinting back and forth between the courts, keeping the ball in play all the time, was to improve judgment, speed and coordination. It was also great for the waistline!

Such strange antics on the courts did not go unnoticed. Nor did the fact that I had signed up for a considerable number of lessons over the remainder of the summer. Suddenly everybody else wanted lessons too. The once-blank pages of Will's appointment book rapidly filled with names. People who had not taken lessons in years signed up for a five-lesson series. Parents signed up their children. Husbands signed up their wives. To accommodate the unexpected spurt in business, Will cut his lunch break in half and added an extra hour at the end of the day. Even that was not enough. By the end of my second week back home, every hour of Will's free time for the remainder of the summer had been booked.

For the first time in the history of the club, people seeking lessons had to be turned away. Many were annoyed at so unprecedented a situation, and as they thumbed disbelievingly through the solidly-penciled pages of Will's appointment book, they quickly singled out the villain. No matter what date they turned to, there was my name monopolizing at least an hour of lesson time, and often two. Nobody seemed to recall that well into midsummer the pages had all been blank.

Will was bewildered by the unexpected run on his services.

"First I had too much time. Now I don't have enough," he said. "If you

threw thousand-dollar bills out there, you could not get some of these people on a court in summer before five o'clock. Now they're fighting each other for a half-hour at noon.

"I don't know whether to thank you," he said with a grin, "or to make you run around the court a hundred times as punishment!"

If the sudden surge of interest in tennis at Gipsy Trail was perplexing to Will, it was the most exciting thing that had happened to the sport at the club as far as Donna and Gordon Fales were concerned. The Fales were definitely not typical of Gipsy Trail tennis.

Donna Floyd Fales had ranked among the top ten women players in

Donna Floyd Fales.

the country through much of the 1960s. She had twice captained victorious Wightman Cup teams and held the number-four spot in women's tennis in the United States when she retired temporarily from national competition the year before to have a baby. Her tall, lanky husband Gordon had ranked among the club's best players since boyhood.

Donna and Gordon loved tennis the way parents love a brilliant but wayward child: their affections, enthusiasms and expectations centered on the sport but they despaired of its weaknesses, particularly at the recreational level. They believed that club tennis, not just at Gipsy Trail but at most clubs, was in drastic need of reshaping and revitalizing, and they heartily endorsed any idea that might spark new life and fresh talent and interest into it. They were the only ones at the club, besides Will, who knew about my tennis experiment. From the beginning, they gave it and me their complete and enthusiastic support.

Some of my strongest support came from people who knew nothing of the experiment but who nevertheless contributed immeasurably to its success because of their deep and genuine love for the sport. There were many times when I wished I could let them in on what I was trying to do, but the decision from the beginning had been to keep the project secret. I especially regretted being unable to take Erza Hartman into my confidence. The *bel esprit* of tennis at Gipsy Trail, this diminutive and dynamic woman is one of the most remarkable people I have ever known.

Erza was already a legend at the club when I first arrived there. For three

generations her word on the courts was law, and her age, like her enormous energy, was the subject of endless speculation. Where tennis was concerned, Erza made the rules, enforced them, established policy, determined (by some method as mysterious as her age) when the courts were playable and who might play upon them, measured nets, selected pros, supervised maintenance and, if necessary, even swept the tapes herself. This was all in addition to the dozen or so other club activities in which she was equally and as enthusiastically involved. That she was able to also play tennis daily from the first day of the season to the last was almost as extraordinary as the fact that she played it so well.

Erza was one of the first people I asked to play with me, and her response was immediate and typical: "Tomorrow morning. Ten o'clock," she said decisively. "One hour will be enough. If you have talent, we work from there. If not, I'll tell you to quit."

I had no doubt that she would. Erza was not one to dissemble.

That first morning session with Erza, and the many that followed, gave me some of my most valuable experience in actual play. I never ceased to be amazed at the patience and effort she put into those games or at her ability on the court. She played the game like a chess player, using her head instead of her feet, running her opponent all over the court while she barely moved from one spot. The speed that had helped her win countless championships over more than sixty years had doubtless slowed by then, but her strategy and placements were still superior to almost anybody's at the club. Erza beat me consistently and soundly, which we both expected, but I learned something from every game and this pleased her as much as it pleased me.

Another of my partners was Peggy Barker, the gal of the Boston accent who had first encountered me on the courts. Peggy was a tall, big-boned red-head who had, on several vacations to

her follow-through was a series of jerks that looked more like furtive waves at a half-recognized friend. But appearances, at least in Peggy's case, meant nothing. What she lacked in style, she made up in skill. Her tennis was excellent.

Like Erza, Peggy played for the pure

The indomitable Erza Hartman.

The unique Hartman backhand.

Puerto Rico, taken lessons from Welby. Watching her play, it was difficult to detect even a single Van Hornism in her form. Her movements on court were clumsy and seemingly uncoordinated. She dropped the racket head on her backswing as if it were weighted, and

pleasure of the sport, which made every game with her a joy. Although she could pick and choose her partners from the best at the club, and did simply by making a phone call, she managed always to find time to fit in a game with me. And she brought the same enthusiasm and interest to our games as she did to those she played with the club champion. When the tournaments began, she came out to warm me up before each match, and then stayed to cheer me on through each contest.

So did Mark T. Walsh, Jr. Mark was then thirteen years old and a head taller than I. His feet were already so big that he could have put a sail on one of his tennis shoes and raced it. Mark did not play in Peggy's or Erza's league—yet. His game was still erratic and unbalanced and his serve, although spectacular, rarely went in more than once every three or four times. But his periodic spurts of brilliance suggested clearly that once he pulled everything together, there would be nobody at the club who could beat him. He proved that last season by winning the Men's Singles Championship at the age of sixteen.

Mark was remarkably graceful for such a huge young man and he moved faster on the court than anyone I had ever seen, including some of the young hot-shots in Puerto Rico. He seemed to be everywhere at once: behind the line, at the net, at one sideline and then the other. It was exhausting to watch him. It was equally exhausting to play with him because the games were so fast, but they forced me to move and that was what I needed.

Occasionally I even managed to take a game from Mark, but it was almost always on his errors. When I did make a point on my own, he was visibly pleased and his exuberant "Hey, that was a good one!" was as rewarding as winning the set.

Thursdays were Ladies' Days at Gipsy Trail. From 9 to 1 P.M. men were barred from the courts while the ladies played what can best be described as

musical tennis courts. The players were divided into A's and B's, the A's theoretically being the better players, although there was always a certain amount of grumbling about who belonged in which category. The decisions were Erza's, and she arrived at them by means that permitted no discussion. Her word was absolute. Each A was then paired with a B, again by some mystical system, and two teams of A's and B's were assigned to each court.

The two teams played five games of doubles, at the end of which the winning pair remained on its original court and the losing pair rotated counterclockwise to the next court. On the new court, the losing pair switched partners with the players already there (i.e., with the winners on that court), and the victorious A teamed up with loser B to play against loser A and victorious B. After several orbits about the courts, every player was supposed to wind up having played with and against every other player. At least that was the way it was supposed to work. It never did. After the second or third rotation, there was always enormous confusion. Some pair inevitably moved when it should have stayed, or switched partners when it should not have, or went clockwise instead of counterclockwise.

The object at the end of the morning was to determine which A and which B had won the most games. (At the end of the season there was a trophy for the high-scoring B and a jovial pat on the back for the high-scoring A who, because of her greater playing skill, was not supposed to require a trophy.) Alas, even the scoring was sometimes so mixed up that only a computer could unscramble it. There was also room, I noticed after several Ladies' Days, for a little manipulation, political or otherwise, at the start of play. The original partner, opposition and court one began with could influence the score somewhat. But over a season, in spite of the tempests and turmoils, Ladies' Days offered a reasonably fair indication of where the women ranked among themselves. (A better gauge would have been a tennis ladder, but attempts over the years to make one work had always failed dismally.) It was also the only chance a great many of the women had to play with the club's prima donnas. Or, for that matter, even to be in the same conversation with them. (Some, of course, never demeaned themselves by turning out for Ladies' Day, but a few, in the manner of great ladies distributing largesse to the poor, did so for the common good of their fellow women.)

Donna had been emphatic about my turning out for Ladies' Day. My first week back, I did not feel that I was ready, particularly since I had not really played any serious games. I was not even sure that I could score properly. She dispatched my misgivings with a wave of the hand.

"The rallying is all fine," she said. "You need it, and plenty of it. But games are a whole new scene. The situation is never the same when you are out there for points. Right now you have to play as many games as you can, and Ladies' Day is a perfect place to start."

That first Ladies' Day was almost as disconcerting as the first doubles game in Puerto Rico. I definitely was not ready for it but I probably would not have been any more ready the following week. When I arrived at the courts, they were already full. I had not seen so many females in a group since my last college reunion. Everybody was warming up at once, and the sight of all those women working out with such concentration was awesome. I did not have a clue to what was going on, nor did anyone offer an explanation. Not that I would have been able to hear it above the animated arguments about who was going to play with whom. I felt sorry for the person who got me.

"Backhand or forehand?" my partner asked when we reached the court.

"I use both," I said.

"How nice," she replied. "Now, what court do you want to play?"

Nobody had ever told me before that I might have a choice. I had always been told: "Stand there." And that is where I had stood. Nor had I been warned about the net. For some reason none of my training had put me even vaguely close to the net. In the informal doubles games I had played in Puerto Rico, all the players had performed from the base lines. One of Welby's major tenets was "play from the back of the court and hit to your opponent's base line." We had concentrated entirely on long, deep balls. At my level of play, this was undoubtedly wise, but unfortunately it left me with no exposure at all to volleying.

Virtually every pro and every book that has been written on the game of doubles in tennis advises the doubles team to play together, either both back or both up at net, depending upon the situation, but the game has almost never been played that way at Gipsy Trail. Another old habit to die hard there, the one-up, one-back position, has managed to resist all efforts to change it by countless coaches over the years. One-up, one-back was the name of the game on Ladies' Day, and "up" was a place I knew instinctively I did not want to be.

But suddenly, there I was, standing 2 feet from the net without a prayer about what to do next. I felt totally exposed and vulnerable. It was soon evident that I was. The opposition took full advantage of my ineptitude. Balls whizzed past me on both sides. One came straight at my face and on reflex I threw up my hands to protect myself. It was hardly the gesture of a Rosie Casals.

Playing in the back position, with my opponent at net, was almost as disconcerting as being there myself. Invariably I returned the serve straight to her and that was the end of the point.

"You'll learn," my partner snapped at me after the fourth such return. She did not sound convinced.

Of the twenty-five games I played on that first memorable Ladies' Day, I was involved in twelve wins and thirteen losses—which speaks well for my partners' perseverance.

After the play, everybody gathered on the terrace overlooking the courts for lunch. The talk was all tennis. For the first time in thirteen years at Gipsy Trail, I understood it. Better still, I was completely engrossed by it!

VI. The Tournament Opens

Donna and Gordon came up from the city for a weekend and, with Will, appraised my progress. They all agreed that it had been considerable, but not nearly enough for the tournaments. They were worried, and with good reason. As Ladies' Day had clearly underlined, I was totally unprepared for net play. My anticipation was still sadly deficient and my reaction time much too slow. In fact, everything I did on the court was too slow. One question haunted me: Was this because of my age or my lack of experience? Had I been ten years younger when the experiment began, would my anticipation and reaction time have been better at this stage of training? In retrospect, I doubt it.

"You are at a stage," Donna said, "when there is no shortcut. You just have to hit balls, and keep hitting them."

"Like how many?" I asked.

"Would you believe five thousand? Maybe ten thousand?"

"How about twenty thousand?" Will added.

That sounded like a lot of balls. I had visions of myself, a little old lady—in tennis shoes of course—still trying to get through the first 10,000. I giggled at the vision. Donna was thoughtful.

"What you really need," she said after a while, "is a Ball Boy machine."

What I really needed was a miracle, but the Ball Boy machine was the next best thing. It could be set to throw drives, volleys, lobs and anything in between, at three speeds and at any angle, but with enough variation on each ball within a set angle that the player had to use footwork in order to hit it. It weighed only 60 pounds, could be moved about easily on its wheels, loaded 40 balls at a time and threw 750 an hour. At that rate, using the machine an hour a day, I could even put Will's 20,000 balls away before the first match of the tournament. By this time I was the proud owner of almost that many.

Where to use the machine was a problem. It required a full tennis court, but to put it on ours, I thought, would cause more attention at the club than I wanted. The ideal place would have been indoors, so that I could use the machine evenings, but I could not find a place close enough to home. At the local sporting goods store I learned of a private clay court not far from the club.

The court belonged to an elderly Bohemian-type opera-singer-artist. He readily agreed to my using the machine on his court, but after an hour's conversation with him, I began having doubts about the wisdom of doing so. Or I should say, after *listening* to him for an hour, since he did all the talking. Like an orator at a country fair he expounded nonstop on his past life, loves and exploits from one continent to another, dragging out an endless supply of scrapbooks, yellowed newspaper clippings and old concert programs. I managed somehow to get the subject back to tennis and this set off a new discourse on the superiority of his tennis skills, the quality of his court, the caliber of the tennis played on it (Wimbledon, at least) and the mediocrity of Gipsy Trail tennis, with which he seemed quite familiar. I was in no position to argue the last but I suspected a certain amount of exaggeration in his earlier statements. I also suspected that instead of being able to practice with the machine, I might be trapped into social games with his friends and instructions from him—all generously offered, no doubt, but not what I was interested in.

The next morning I brought over the machine with no commitments other than to give it a try. To my dismay, the court, which I had not seen the day before, was surfaced with what looked like river-bottom ooze. It was down in a hollow, surrounded by mosquito-filled bushes, and its lines were marked with bits and pieces of chalk, lime, pebbles and various unidentifiable objects. As I suspected, my host had thoughtfully provided me with a partner—an octogenarian at least—and, for good measure, both he and his wife were also dressed to play. Their outfits were straight from the 1920s. I felt as if I had stumbled upon some outdoor set for *Arsenic and Old Lace*.

For an hour and a half I listened patiently to a running commentary on what was wrong with my form, stroke and game while all three took turns showing me how the game should be played. (Welby would not have believed it.) When I was finally able to get the machine set up in the mud, it was to a dogmatic denunciation of all machines as worthless. (I am sure this fellow still went to bed grumbling about the horseless carriage.) As if to prove his theories, the Ball Boy machine threw half a dozen balls and quit.

The problem turned out to be nothing more serious than a connection that had joggled loose in transport, but happily it gave me an excuse to load the machine back into the car and take it home to Gipsy Trail, which was, after all, the only practical place to use it.

The Ball Boy machine was not intended as a gimmick nor as a substitute for actual game play. What it did offer was the opportunity to compress into a brief period of time experience that might otherwise have taken years to acquire. Every shot which might ever occur in a game could be duplicated and repeated endlessly on the machine. I learned to volley with it by hitting so many balls that I developed blisters on my calluses. I improved my placements by returning hundreds of balls to colored Hula Hoops which we put down in various places on the opposite courts. Will would shout "yellow" or "red" and I would try to place the ball in the circle of that color.

Somewhere between the 10,000th and the 20,000th ball, I began to be able to predict where the next ball was going before it crossed the net to my side. Once I was able to do that, I was able to move into position to hit it *before* the ball reached the strike zone, instead of trying to run to it after it was already there. It was a tremendous breakthrough. To people who have played the game all their lives, this sounds like nothing. But it was one of the simple basic intangibles no one could teach me. They could talk about it, but I could not translate the message into action. It was something I could learn only with experience. As Donna had said, there were no shortcuts.

There were times when, with the Ball Boy throwing balls without letup and Donna and Will both working on me at once to do this or stop doing that, I felt I was caught in the eye of a hurricane; and others when I had the strange sensation that I was watching the whole scene from a distance while some Pavlovian puppet was responding to the commands.

But I *was* responding, and that was what mattered. The exercises and drills had definitely improved my speed and reactions. I was playing with more confidence and even a hint of authority. By the third Ladies' Day I was high-score among the B's, two games better than the next best score. I tried to act casual at lunch but I was exploding inside.

"Why don't you sign up for the tournament?" Erza said, congratulating me. "It's good practice for you."

I mumbled something vague and tried to change the subject. There were still a couple of days until entries closed. Donna and Gordon had hoped to keep my name off the tournament list until the last moment to postpone the flak they knew the announcement of my entry, and particularly of my partners, would create at the club.

Gordon had volunteered to be my Mixed Doubles partner. Since he nor-

mally played in the tournament each year, both he and Donna felt that his playing with me was valid to the experiment. We all agreed that Donna, who never played in the tournament because she could beat everybody—male and female—at the club, was out of the question as my partner for Ladies' Doubles. Victory with Gordon would still require effort and some ability on my part; victory with Donna would be so one-sided that it would prove nothing as far as the experiment was concerned. (It would also have put us both out looking for another club.)

For Ladies' Doubles, Donna and Gordon asked Mary Connorton, a pretty, young second-grade teacher at St. David's, to be my partner. Mary played excellent tennis and managed to avoid the entanglements of the court clique while remaining on happy terms with all its intimates. That she cheerfully accepted their request knowing nothing of the experiment but a good deal about my skill says something about Mary's good sportsmanship.

Once Erza began on the subject of the tournament there was no way I could keep the news, or at least part of it, quiet any longer. After insisting before the assembled group that I sign up, she then insisted that one of the poorest B players, who was a relative newcomer to the club, sign up with me. I had no choice but to tell her that I already had a partner for Ladies' Doubles. When she heard that it was Mary Connorton, the change in her expression was instant. Her smile dissolved into a look of shock. She stared at me, speechless, as if in a sudden flash of intuition she was seeing all too clearly the monster she had helped create.

There was a deadly silence among the other ladies. The poor woman Erza had been trying to talk into being my partner was thoroughly confused.

"Is there a rule that B players are not allowed to play in the tournament with A players?" she asked in a small voice.

"There is no rule," Erza snapped, "but why would any A want to play with a B?" It was a good question.

From the chill at lunch it was clear that I had gone too far. With Mary Connorton as my partner, there was a reasonable chance that I might get beyond the first round. What was worse, I had altered the absolute predictability of the tournament. There is no place for the unpredictable at Gipsy Trail. It was almost frightening to contemplate the effect my signing up with Donna would have had.

The effect of my signing up with Gordon was dramatic enough. He entered our names on the Mixed Doubles list fifteen minutes before the deadline on the Saturday of the draw. He then walked to the clubhouse for lunch. Within minutes five people had rushed to the dining room to ask if the news was true. Gordon chewed on a bacon-and-tomato sandwich and kept his cool. Will met me an hour later on the court and said: "The word is 'poor Gordon!' " I could not help but agree.

All matches in the first round of the Labor Day tournaments had to be played within a week of the draw. My schedule was Ladies' Singles on Friday, Ladies' Doubles on Saturday, and Mixed Doubles on Sunday.

"You might as well leave town on Monday," my husband said, "because you are going to fall flat on your face." All through the summer he had watched my efforts with a cold eye, neither approving nor disapproving. His ungallant comments now were infuriating.

"Would you like to bet?" I said in a flush of pretournament bravado.

He not only took me on, but by the end of the week was mentally counting his winnings. Each trip to the courts, where I worked out in those final days with a vengeance, only made him laugh harder.

Donna spent the last day with me working on my serve and strategy. The object of both was to get the ball over the net . . . period. I could count on Mary and Gordon to carry me through most of the games I played with them, but in singles I was strictly on my own. My own, alas, was still pretty poor. I was not ready to do more than keep the ball in play, but that was half the battle. If I concentrated solely on getting the ball across the net to my opponent, then it was a better than even chance that she would make the error and lose the point. More games than most people realize are won in just this way.

I was awake most of the night before the match, my mind a kaleidoscope through which the fragmented bits and pieces of the previous weeks whirled in dizzying confusion. It was ridiculous to be so unstrung by a sport. After all, I kept reminding myself, this was only a game. The thought was of little comfort.

The match went three sets. I lost the first 1–6. It was a psychologically exhausting contest. My opponent played a maddening but steady lob-game, sending shot after shot so high into the air they were almost out of sight. I lobbed back until I could stand the frustration no longer. Then I tried putting the ball away with a smash or a drop-shot. Since neither of these shots was in my limited repertoire, my opponent inevitably took the point. The more points she took, the more exasperated I became. It finally dawned upon me that this was *her* strategy. It was working beautifully.

In the second set I resigned myself to outsteadying her if it took the rest of the day. It took forty minutes, but I won 6–1. Then I missed two easy backhands in the first game of the third set and my newfound confidence collapsed. My strokes deteriorated into tentative, paceless shots and I was again on the defensive. By the end of the seventh game the score was 3–4 and the situation looked hopeless.

As we changed sides, I glanced at the gallery. My husband was ruffling through a handful of bills as if counting his winnings. It was exactly what I needed to snap me back to reality. Everything I seemed to have forgotten in those last few minutes came back. I took the next three games and won the match. It was as far as I got in singles, but under the circumstances, it was a giant step.

The victory was short-lived. Even Mary Connorton's fine playing could not carry me through Ladies' Doubles. Predictably, our opponents played to me, and predictably, I flubbed. We lost the match 4–6, 6–2, 2–6.

I spent another sleepless night worrying this time about poor Gordon. As it turned out, I need not have. Neither our first nor second opponents were any match for him, with or without me. He gave up only three games in two rounds. We made it—or rather, Gordon made it —to the semifinals. If we could win this one and reach the finals, then regardless of the outcome, the experiment could surely be considered a success.

Cocktail-lounge quotes on the odds against our winning the semifinals were 40–60. We faced the incumbent champions—the indomitable Erza Hartman and Ken Scott—the most formidable doubles team at Gipsy Trail. Now it was really time to say "poor Gordon."

Erza and Ken had taken the Mixed Doubles title five times in the previous seven years. In reaching the semifinals they had played one of the most dramatic matches of the season, a three-set contest which lasted almost three hours and had them at match point ten times. Ken's game was strong, steady and always clever. Although he was well into his fifties, he had won the Men's Singles Championship three times in the previous four years, twice defeating Gordon for the title. Like Erza, his superb placements, vast experience and brilliant strategy more than made up for his opponents' advantage in age. He could demolish kids a third his age by running them all over the court. We had no illusions about this match.

Every doubles game I played that week was mentally played against Erza and Ken. There were tall Erzas and Kens and short ones, fat ones and thin ones, blond ones and brunettes. They came in combinations of sexes, sizes and skills. One afternoon Erza was a tall, bespectacled male member. By chance one of my returns caught him off balance and I shouted: "Take that, Erza!" I turned around to see the real Erza peering strangely at me through the windscreen.

The gallery began gathering for the match a full hour before game time. It was the largest turnout of the season and there was an air of excitement on the courts. The real Erza and Ken played masterfully, and the applause was frequent and genuine. But Gordon was the star and he was brilliant. He was everywhere at once, long arms and legs flailing about like a windmill. But surprisingly, I was in a few places nobody expected me to be too. For once I contributed at least something to the partnership. We won the match 8–6, 6–4.

Everything afterwards was anticlimactic. Ironically, our opponents in the finals were Mary Connorton and her brother Kevin. Just as Gordon and I had been *on* the day before, Mary and Kevin were *on* that day. They played magnificent tennis. We were no match for them. It was the right way for the tournament to end.

"Besides," my husband said, poorer but friendlier, "I was thinking of asking you to play doubles with me next year. If you had won, you would probably turn me down!" It was the right way for the experiment to end too.

VII. End of the Experiment

A friend once remarked that when I die the inscription on my tombstone should read: "Never did anything in moderation that could be done to excess." Certainly this applies to the way I learned to play tennis. But equally true is the fact that I *did* learn to play in a single season, and while my skill was limited, it was sufficient to enable me to play an acceptable club-level game in reasonable comfort both with the sport and with my partners. That was, after all, the basic goal of the experiment, and as such, it was decidedly a success.

More important, my unorthodox approach to tennis at a time when the current and still-growing boom had not yet begun unquestionably sparked new life, interest and enthusiasm into the game at Gipsy Trail. It encouraged a number of adults to play who might otherwise have been relegated forever, as I had been, to sitting on the sidelines because they had not been raised with tennis rackets in their hands.

But looking back on that summer, there are certain fundamental lessons to be learned from the experience. The first and most obvious is that too much of anything can be as bad as not enough. The staggering number of hours and the all-encompassing effort to learn the game, particularly in those first few weeks, were actually self-defeating. Admittedly the problem with my ankles was the result of a freak accident, but even without that the overall effect of such effort was debilitating physically and psychologically. What should have been fun was often work, and considering the snail's pace of my progress, not very rewarding work at that. An hour's lesson a day, and at the most two more of assorted drills and practices, particularly in the early stages, would probably have yielded as much or more progress in the same duration. Later, when I was better conditioned physically and had a broader grasp of the fundamentals, this could have been increased—but never to the point where it ceased to be enjoyable. Sport, after all, is supposed to be fun.

Nor do I believe, in retrospect, that Welby's teaching approach was nearly as successful with me as it is with children. I am referring now not to the technique he taught but to the method he used to teach it. Certainly his outstanding record with youngsters speaks for itself, and certainly the raw material he was working with in me was far below that of his junior protégés. But methods that work with children do not necessarily work with adults. I was long past the age where the crack-on-the-knuckles kind of psychology was very effective. Or perhaps it was simply a matter of personality. Whatever the reason, I cannot help but feel that I, and a great many people like me, respond to praise more positively than to criticism. Welby's constant badgering did not make me love him or the sport more. It merely resigned me to enduring them both.

Much more significant is my feeling that group lessons in the early stages would have worked more efficiently than private ones. There is a definite place for the latter and there always will be. At certain stages, only private instruction can work out a particular problem or help move a player from one plateau to the next. But I am convinced it is a decided advantage for beginners of any age to be able to measure their progress against that of others, as well as to mutually commiserate. This has long been recognized with children, but not with adults, although adults, too, seem to move ahead faster, especially in the early stages of learning, when working alongside others. By group I do not mean a mob but a limited and manageable number, all on the same general skill level.

Four or six or eight students, all starting out together from scratch, create their own incentives to learning. Although it is doubtful if anyone ever exhibited less ability at a sport than I did at tennis, it would nevertheless have been encouraging to recognize that other adults had problems too. Having

those superperfect teen-age prodigies playing world-class-level tennis all around me while I struggled just to hit the ball did little for my morale.

Nor did the climate, nor the isolation from home, friends and familiar surroundings. Obviously my case was extreme since people do not normally take up a sport by going off for five weeks of virtual solitary confinement—which is the way I shall always think of those weeks in San Juan, at least socially. But people often do take up a sport while away from home on vacation or business. A word of wisdom: Do not take up tennis in the tropics in summer. The conditions are totally unsuitable for tackling any sport that requires one or more hours of running around on a steamy surface. The Caribe courts took their toll of my meager resources.

So much for the things I would have done differently. There are a lot of things I would have done exactly the same. Heading that list is the solid foundation of strokes and style that I acquired from Welby. I suffered to acquire it, no question, but several years and countless games later I can honestly say that it was all worthwhile. Welby gave me something to grow from, not instantly, overnight, as I would have liked, but steadily and surely. In the long run, this is the best kind of growth.

My experiment was a success but it also proved that there is no shortcut to the game. Perhaps more than any other popularly played sport, tennis is a game of skill and experience. This explains its tremendous attraction and durability. One can acquire the rudimentary skills in a brief period but only experience improves their function.

The regimen of initial skills that Welby Van Horn teaches is what makes his particular game of tennis distinctive. This distinction shows best in his young superstars, but it is evident too in his less gifted protégés. Even the nonathletic, uncoordinated, middle-aged player looks a little better on the courts using Welby Van Horn's style of tennis.

In the chapters that follow are many of the techniques Welby teaches, along with a potpourri of additional advice from other talented and dedicated professionals, all designed to make tennis players out of undistinguished, as well as distinguished, athletes.

PART II: Instruction

VIII. Balance and Grip

If you are going to drive a car, you start out with a car. If you are going to sail, you start with a boat. But if you are going to learn to play tennis, you do not necessarily begin on a tennis court with racket and balls. In fact, this is probably the least desirable way to attack the sport, but convincing a beginner of this, particularly if he is an adult, takes a certain amount of doing. Adults are anxious to get on with the game and many consider preliminary exercises more time-consuming than valuable. They *are* time-consuming, but they *are* valuable, and there is no way to get around either truth.

Understandably, an adult coming late to the sport wants to use any short-cut he can to make up for mileage already lost. In skiing, there is the Graduated Length Method of teaching which starts a beginner out on abbreviated skis and then moves him from one length to the next as he progresses from plateau to plateau. The system works, dramatically. You can find people on any hill in America these days paralleling through slalom gates as if they had done so all their lives who, except for the Graduated Length Method, would still be struggling through the snow-plow. But unfortunately there is no Graduated Length Method in tennis. If there were, I assure you I would have found it a long time ago. The only genuine road to tennis is a sound foundation. As boring and frustrating as this may be to acquire, it is the only way to build a dependable game.

You *can* go out and hit balls. You *can* start right out with play. You may hit some of the balls and get them over the net. If you have a natural aptitude for ball sports and your eye-hand coordination is good, you may even be able to muddle your way through games. But the fellow who does this is a loser. He loses, first, because he will never play more than a slipshod game, and second, because he has obviously wasted an innate tennis talent which with proper training could have been developed into a winning game.

Not surprisingly, it is even more important for an adult beginner to concentrate on the fundamentals than it is for a youngster, because the adult has less time in which to develop his skills. He must put everything he learns to work for him as quickly as possible for the most productive results. And he must do so with the least embarrassment to himself in front of his playing companions. It is only common sense, then, that his foundation be of concrete, not sand; that it be solid enough to build upon and expand, and durable enough to withstand aging and declining physical ability. A really solid foundation, such as is taught by Welby Van Horn and many other respected professionals, is all these things. Although he may not be able to translate it immediately into winning games, it will ensure the beginner faster progress and greater long-range rewards than any other approach to the sport.

The four major elements of a sound tennis foundation are: (1) balance; (2) grip; (3) stroke; and (4) strategy —*in that order*. As Welby emphasized in my first practice lesson with him, there is no way to employ *strategy* in tennis unless you can first control the ball. There is no way to control the ball without first having command of the proper *strokes* with which to do so. Such strokes depend on using the proper *grips* on the rackets, and then upon the action of the entire body in using the racket. Since the action of the body is dependent upon *balance*, this is the point at which any tennis training must begin. The sequence is logical and practical.

Balance

Leave your racket at home for the basic lessons in balance. In fact, *you* can stay home too since this exercise is better practiced before a full-length mirror in your bedroom than on a tennis court. If you do not have a full-length mirror and you do not mind a quizzical glance or two from passersby, any plate-glass store window in which you can see your reflected image will do just as well.

Balance is a major factor in determining how gracefully, or awkwardly, one performs various physical actions. There are no sports, and few physical activities for that matter, which do not place a high premium upon balance. Horseback riding, skiing, golf, bicycling, dancing, even the simple climbing of stairs, all involve balance in one form or another. Although the types of balance may differ from activity to activity, perfect balance produces maximum performance with minimum effort. It is what makes a baseball player hit a home run seemingly without effort; or a figure skater execute an intricate jump with ease. It is an essential ingredient of power in tennis, more so than physical size or strength. Yet it is one of the least studied, most often misunderstood elements in playing good tennis. Remember this when you are tempted to skip these initial exercises.

The three parts of the body that are the major keys to balance in tennis, and in virtually all movements, are the head, hips and heels. How the Three H's, as they are called, interrelate is something you can check and correct by yourself. This is why you need the mirror.

For the forehand balance, stand sideways to the mirror, which represents the net, with your left side to it and your feet planted flat and about the same distance apart as the width of your shoulders. Take a step towards the mirror, shifting your weight squarely onto your left foot and planting it at about a 30-degree angle to the mirror. (The

b) Transfer weight to forward or anchor foot, pivoting on rear toe.

Forehand Balance: a) Begin with feet sideways and parallel to net, body turned as shown.

c) With arms hanging loosely at sides, rotate body to face net.

use of *left* and *right* in this exercise and in all subsequent ones applies to a right-handed player. A left-handed player, obviously, should reverse the procedures.) You will notice that in stepping forward and transferring your weight onto your left foot, it is necessary to lift the heel of your right foot and pivot on your right toe, thus rotating your body towards the mirror. Your arms, which have been hanging loosely at your sides, are still in that position, but your hips and shoulders are now parallel to the mirror. Your left foot still remains planted firmly in position. This is your *anchor* foot, and its purpose is exactly that: to anchor your weight, steady your body and balance your movement. Your right foot, which is your *adjustment* foot, does all the work by permitting your entire body to pivot on it.

The last stage of this exercise is to bring your body erect, feet still in position, with knees flexed and shoulders and hips level. Depending upon the amount of knee flex, which should be comfortable but not extreme, your right hip may be slightly higher than your left.

Throughout the exercise, your head should be level, and at the end should be positioned directly above your anchor foot. Welby has rightly observed that the position of the head in golf is stressed *ad nauseum* but that it is rarely if ever discussed in tennis. He considers it at least as important in tennis as in golf and is so emphatic about keeping the head level in the forehand and backhand balance positions that he often has his students practice the exercises with a book on their heads, or in extreme cases, with a water-filled glass. Before you decide this is silly, try it. If

you still think it silly, be grateful at least that you are working in the privacy of your own home.

Do this exercise at least a dozen times, until you get the feeling of the weight transfer as you rotate your body and pivot on your adjustment foot. Each time, check visually in the mirror that your head, hips and heels are all in proper position, that your knees are flexed and that your torso is erect. You should feel relaxed and steady. If you are weaving about like a Saturday night drunk, one of the Three H's is off. Check your anchor foot. Is it angled correctly to the mirror? Is your head level and positioned above it? Are you up on the toes of your adjustment foot or still flat on your heel? Is all of your weight forward? Have you rotated shoulders but not hips? Any of these will throw off your balance. Of course, if it *is* Saturday night and you are a little drunk that will do it too!

It is a good idea to thoroughly perfect the forehand balance exercises before tackling the backhand exercises. This is not because the backhand is more difficult. It is not. Contrary to what most beginners believe, the backhand is actually a more natural stroke than the forehand since you are swinging *away* from your body instead of *across it*. But because each new element at this preliminary training stage creates new confusion, it is better to master one element at a time.

There is not a great deal of difference between the exercises for backhand and forehand balance. In the backhand, as in the forehand, begin by standing sideways to the mirror, this time with your right side to it. As you step forward on your right foot, plant your anchor at a 45-degree angle to the mirror instead of

b) With anchor foot at 45-degree angle to net, transfer weight forward.

Backhand balance: a) As in forehand balance, begin by standing sideways to net with right hip forward.

c) As body rotates, right hip drops slightly lower than left.

at the 30-degree angle used in the forehand. The difference is because in taking the racket back on a backhand, the body turns more than it does on a forehand, but in rotating forward for the stroke and follow-through, it turns less. For this reason, the adjustment, or left foot, on which the body pivots also moves less. With less forward rotation, you should have a greater feeling of leaning in and towards the mirror. This will drop your right hip slightly lower than your left at the completion of the exercise.

It is just as important in the backhand as in the forehand that your head remain level throughout the exercise, and that at the end it is positioned above your anchor foot. Check this and the other H's each time you practice the backhand balance, and do this one too until you feel completely familiar with it. Console yourself for the effort by the thought that it is not only invaluable preparation for the basic ground strokes but also great for the waistline.

Grip

Show a gun collector a new or antique or simply unfamiliar firearm and the first thing he will do is pick it up, turn it every which way for minute inspection, weigh its balance and feel, hoist it to shooting position and, for lack of more descriptive terminology, fondle it. He is getting its feel. Much of the satisfaction, understanding and familiarity a collector derives from handling a firearm can be experienced by the would-be tennis player with a racket.

All rackets are not alike. Each has its own particular characteristics of balance, weight, feel and general esthetics. Before undertaking any exercises with a racket, the beginner should simply handle it. How he handles it is unimportant. The object is to become familiar with it, to get to know it, to feel comfortable with it. Leave it about the house for a few days and pick it up whenever you notice it. Hold it in your hands while you are watching the evening news on TV. Grasp it loosely at the throat with your left hand and twirl the handle with your right. Using your thumb and middle finger, hold the end of the handle and let the racket swing, head down, back and forth. You will be surprised at how soon the racket begins to feel a part of you. Once it does, you are ready to learn the formal grips.

The stroke most often used in tennis is the forehand drive. The grip most often used for the forehand drive by both professionals and amateurs is known as the Eastern forehand grip. The Eastern forehand grip, in contrast to other grips, provides the most power and the greatest control over the ball. It is also the most natural, and therefore the most logical, grip with which to hit a forehand drive. You can test this for yourself in front of the mirror by imagining that you are going to hit a ball towards the net with the palm of your hand. To do so, obviously you would not angle your palm down towards the floor, or up towards the ceiling. Now if you imagine that the face of the racket is actually an extension of your palm, as the racket itself is an extension of your arm, you will then understand the Eastern grip.

To take an Eastern forehand grip on the racket, hold the racket loosely at the throat in your left hand with the face perpendicular to the floor. Now extend

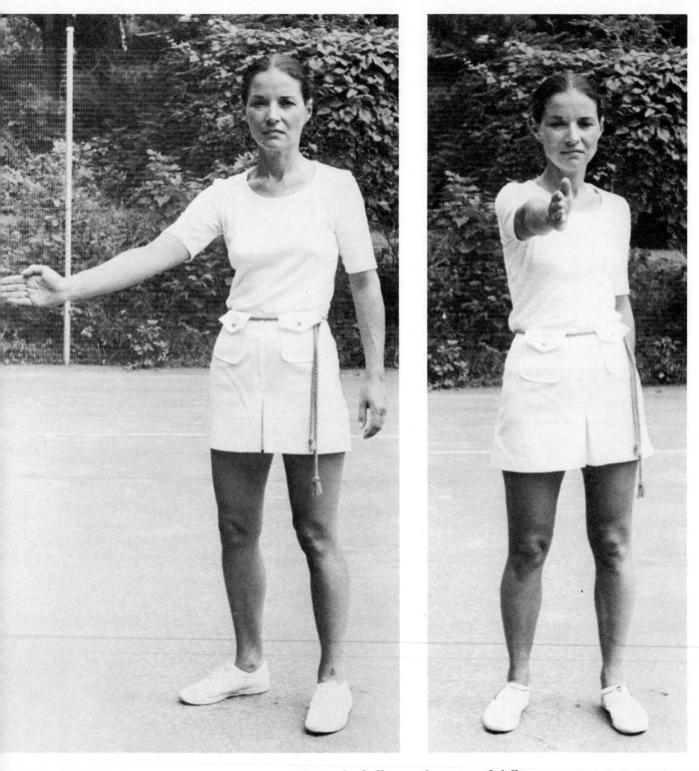

Hitting the ball over the net, and follow-
through, with palm of hand.

your palm as you did to hit that imaginary ball, and wrap your fingers and thumb about midway down the leather grip on the racket, with your thumb positioned between your index and middle finger. The knuckle of your index finger should be on the right side of the handle. Your palm and the face of the racket should be on the same plane, both perpendicular to the floor. This is often called "shaking hands with the racket," and that is a good description of what you do when you grasp it in your hand.

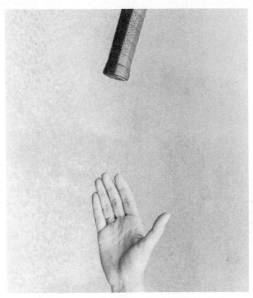

For Eastern forehand grip, hold racket loosely at throat with left hand, and extend right hand, palm open, as if to hit an imaginary ball.

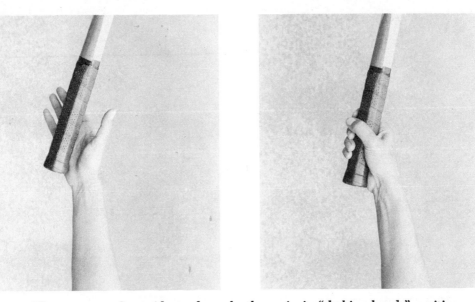

Then grasp racket midway down leather grip in "shaking hands" position. When hand is closed, thumb is positioned between index and middle finger.

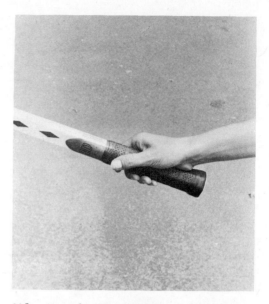

Side view of correct Eastern forehand grip.

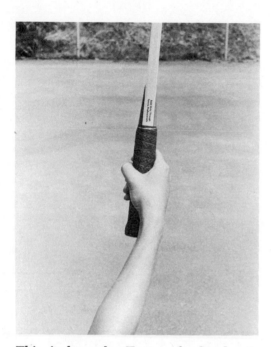

This is how the Eastern forehand grip should look to you.

In incorrect grip, hand is rotated forward.

Your grip on the handle should be firm and the racket should feel comfortably secure in your hand. If it is too loose, it will twist out of your grip at the first contact with the ball. But if it is a stranglehold, as mine was in the initial stages of training, it will actually restrict your circulation and cramp the muscles of your hand so that you will not be able to hit balls at all. It is not a bad thought to remind yourself from time to time that a racket is a stringed instrument more closely related to a violin than to a baseball bat. It should be handled with a firm but sensitive touch. The great Don Budge was said to have such a delicate touch that even the leather grip on his handle interfered with his ability to "feel" the racket. He always removed the leather grips and held on to the bare wood. Since you are not that sensitive (if you are, you should not be reading this book), leave the leather grip on your racket until it gets so cruddy that it has to be replaced; then replace it. It provides a much more solid gripping area on the handle than bare wood and prevents the racket from becoming slippery when your hand perspires.

Most tennis players grip the racket handle close to its end or butt, which is where it is meant to be gripped. But for the beginner, it is easier to control both the racket and the ball if you grip the handle about midway. No matter where on the handle you grip it, your wrist should be straight, your fingers and thumb should be properly positioned, and at no time should the butt end of the handle touch your wrist. If it does, you are definitely doing something wrong. Go back and read this section again.

The Eastern forehand grip is also the "ready" grip since this is the way you will hold your racket while waiting for a ball from the opposite court. If the ball is one you will return with a forehand, your grip remains the same as you pivot your body to the right. If the ball requires a backhand, the grip must be altered slightly. Again, your palm will give you an idea of why. With your hand pointed at the mirror in front of you, palm at right angles to the floor, move your hand across your body and back towards your left shoulder as you would to make a backhand shot. Note that as your hand approaches your left shoulder, your palm angles down slight-

To understand backhand grip, note position of palm in backhand movement.

ly towards the floor. Now repeat the same movement with the racket in your hand, using the Eastern forehand grip. Note that the racket as it approaches your left shoulder tilts, as your palm tilted, towards the floor. It is no longer perpendicular. If you were to hit a ball with the net side of the racket face at this angle (backhands are hit on one side of the strings, forehands on the other), the ball would travel towards the ceiling instead of towards the net. You must therefore make an adjustment in the grip in order to keep the racket face perpendicular to the floor.

To make this adjustment, return to the ready position, holding the racket

Backhand grip is demonstrated by standing racket on edge and grasping handle as if to pick up. Your hand automatically assumes Eastern backhand grip (below).

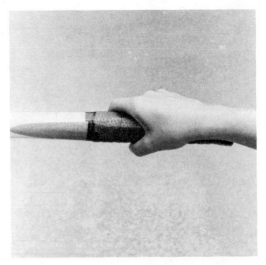

Another view of correct backhand grip.

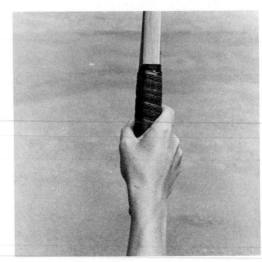

How it looks to you.

Ready Position—forward and side views. Note position of left and right hands on racket.

with the Eastern forehand grip. Relax your fingers on the handle. With your left hand cradling the throat of the racket, guide the racket head about one-eighth turn to the *right*. At the same time, slide your right hand about one-eighth turn to the *left* on the racket handle. Remember: the left hand guides, the right hand slides. The knuckle of your index finger will now have moved from a position on the right side of the handle to a position almost on top of it. If it is directly on top of the racket handle, you have shifted too far to the left. Shift back slightly. In the Eastern backhand position, fingers and thumb should be positioned just as they were for the forehand. Some beginners feel greater confidence with their backhand grip if they extend their right thumb along the handle of the racket.

It is not incorrect to do so with the backhand grip (it is with the forehand), so try both thumb positions and settle for which feels more comfortable.

Again using the mirror, there is a positive way to check on whether or not your grips are correct. Stand in the ready position with the racket at right angles to the mirror and the strings perpendicular to the floor. Now rotate halfway to the right so that the racket is parallel to the mirror. Your racket face should still be perpendicular to the floor if your Eastern forehand grip is correct. Return to the ready position, shift to the Eastern backhand grip and rotate halfway to the left so that your racket is again parallel to the mirror. If your racket face is not perpendicular to the floor but the hitting side is angled slightly upwards, you have not adjusted your grip far enough to the left on the handle.

A word about the ready position. In this position, it is very important that your grip on the racket handle be relaxed. Your left hand holds the racket at the throat, ready to guide it. The fingers of the right hand must be loose enough on the handle to quickly and effortlessly slide to the backhand grip if the ball is a backhand. In both the backhand and the forehand, your grip should remain relaxed until just before the racket makes contact with the ball. Only then should your entire hand tighten on the racket. A trick is to say to yourself "squeeze" just before hitting the ball.

Many beginners experience unnecessary difficulty shifting from the forehand to the backhand positions simply because they have such a death-grip on the racket that they cannot let it go in time to make the change. Again, think of the violin. You would not hold it like a club. The same applies to your racket.

The Eastern forehand and backhand grips are the basic ones you will need for most strokes in tennis. But you will not feel like a bona fide tennis player unless you also know what is meant by a Continental grip and a Western grip. For years, tennis professionals have expounded a lot of mumbo-jumbo on these grips which makes them sound complicated and mysterious. The only

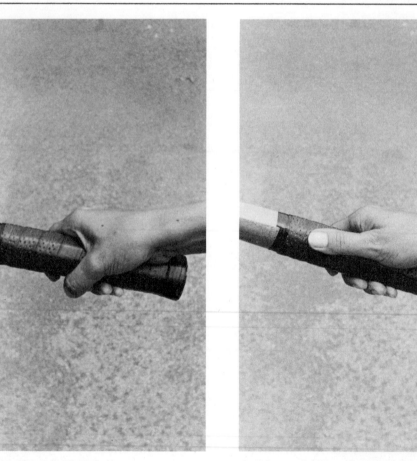

Continental grip—thumb in.   Continental grip—thumb along handle.

Western grip is achieved by placing racket flat on ground.

When racket is gripped, "V" of hand is on flat side of handle.

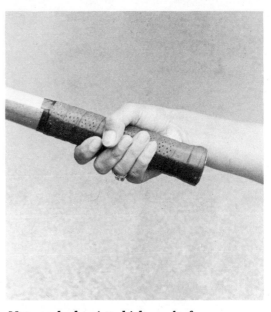

Note arched wrist which results from Western grip.

thing they really are is superfluous. There is actually very little difference between a Continental grip and an Eastern backhand grip, and whatever that difference is would be indistinguishable to anyone but an expert. If you were to hit a forehand drive using your Eastern backhand grip, this would best describe the Continental grip. Although England's Fred Perry became one of tennis's greats using the Continental grip, it is unlikely to do anything for the average beginner's game except make it worse. Try hitting a forehand with the backhand grip and you will quickly see why. The strain placed upon the wrist is tremendous. The only time that the Continental grip makes any sense at all is at net, when the play is often too fast to permit the luxury of changing grips. Then a modification somewhere between the backhand and the forehand grips will permit you to volley both backhand and forehand balls without switching.

The weirdest grip to watch is the Western. It originated in California and an occasional player still uses it to smash hard overheads down into the opposite court. For almost any other stroke, it is awkward, clumsy and easily exploitable. To arrive at a Western grip, lay the racket flat on the ground. Now grip the handle to pick it up. You will find that the "V" formed by your thumb and forefinger is now on the flat side of the handle rather than on the narrow side. In order to hit a forehand with this grip, it is necessary to arch the wrist, which is asking for more trouble than any beginner can afford. The backhand with this grip is even more astounding since there is no way to hit the ball, holding the racket in this position, on the other side of the strings. This means that the racket is turned over so that the backhand and forehand balls are hit off the same side of the strings. A Western-grip player switching from forehand to backhand drives looks as if he is either waving to a friend in the stands or swatting bees on the court.

Now that you know about the Con-tinental and Western grips, you can safely forget them. The only other grip you will have to master is the service grip, and until you have graduated from beginner to intermediate, the best all-around service grip is the Eastern fore-hand, with the one simple modification of extending the forefinger along the racket handle for more power and con-trol. As you progress, your grip can also progress somewhat towards the Eastern backhand, again with the forefinger ex-tended. This permits greater snap and flexibility for the wrist, which in the serve (as you will learn later in chap-ter XII) is important. But until you mas-ter a consistent, flat serve with the East-ern forehand, do not confuse yourself with an additional service grip.

Concentrate on a proper, comfortable Eastern forehand and Eastern back-hand and you will be able to handle all the shots you are likely to encounter in your first few years of play.

IX. The Forehand and Backhand

The game of tennis involves three basic kinds of strokes: ground strokes, volleys and overheads. Ground strokes are all those that are made after the ball has bounced on your side of the net. These include the forehand and backhand drives, the lob, the drop-shot and the half-volley, which in spite of its name is not a true volley since it is hit after the ball has bounced. True volleys, which get their name from the French *voler*, meaning *to fly*, are balls hit in flight *before* they bounce on your side of the net. There are both forehand and backhand volleys as well as drop volleys and lob volleys. Overheads, as the name implies, are strokes made when the ball is actually over your head. The most common overhead stroke is the serve; the most spectacular, the overhead smash.

Of all these strokes, the three most important to a beginner are the forehand and backhand drives and the serve. In fact, one West Coast coach suggests that the only two strokes a beginner needs to play are the forehand drive and the serve. He could even play with only one stroke by eliminating the overhead serve altogether. It is legal, al-though not common, in most club-level play to substitute a forehand drive hit off a hand-bounced ball for a conventional overhead serve. But neither of us is suggesting this and there would be little reason to read this book if the game of tennis could be reduced to a single stroke.

What I am trying to emphasize is the importance of the forehand drive and the serve in relation to other strokes in the game. If you have ever watched the National matches at Forest Hills or the championships at Wimbledon, you will certainly agree on the importance of the serve, but you may wonder about the forehand drive. In men's tennis, particularly, it is becoming a disappearing art. But this is true only in big-time tournament tennis where the game is about as much like club-level social tennis as an Eldorado is like a Volkswagen. The genus is the same, but the subspecies is vastly disparate.

Now that anybody can have big-time tournament tennis in his living room just by turning on the television set, the difference between the two kinds of play has created considerable confusion in the minds of many social players.

Forehand Drive: a) **In ready position body is square to net, racket is pointed forward.** b) **Keeping strings perpendicular to ground, turn sideways to net.**

With the professionals, there is no question that the big serve, followed by a charge to the net and a smashing putaway, overrides all other strokes. With such dramatic shots in one's repertoire, there is no need to depend upon drives. This, unfortunately, has misled a great many novices into thinking that ground strokes have gone out of style. They may have at Wimbledon, but they definitely have not at the local club.

The number of social players, even at top club level, capable of playing the big-time serve-and-smash game of the professionals—consistently—is very small indeed, and they are doubtless wasting their time and talents hanging around your club. The basis of good tennis for the average player is not spectacular, and usually undependable, glamour strokes but sound, solid ground strokes. For this reason a beginner should not even think about any other stroke until he has thoroughly mastered his forehand and backhand drives so that he can put the ball over the net and deep to his opponent's base line with control and consistency.

Forehand Drives

The reason for all those forehand balance exercises will be clear as soon as you begin hitting forehand drives. But do not open the can of balls yet. There are some forehand drive exercises to try first. Again, you can do these best in front of your mirror but it is a good idea to move the lamps and bric-a-brac out of the way. Begin by holding the racket in the ready position, pointed at the mirror, its butt at your stomach and its

c) Backswing is complete when racket is even with shoulders and behind you.

d) Racket head drops slightly and racket moves forward as body pivots and weight shifts onto anchor foot.

head angled slightly upwards. Keep the strings perpendicular to the floor and step back with your right foot, turning sideways to the mirror as you did for the forehand balance exercises. As you do, bring your racket back so that it is even with your shoulders and winds up pointing directly behind you, its head angled upwards, strings still perpendicular to the floor. This is your backswing. In making it, your hips and shoulders should move at the same time and together. If your shoulders turn more than your hips, your backswing will be too long. You will then be slowed down when you bring your racket forward.

Now, rotating your body exactly as you did in the forehand balance exercise, bring the racket forward as your body pivots and your weight shifts onto the left foot. Watch in the mirror what happens to the racket as you complete

the backswing and initiate the forward motion. If your racket head jiggles about, or twists so that its face angles up or down instead of remaining perpendicular to the floor, or looks as if it is a waving flag, you have a problem. It is not an uncommon one. The next time you are on court, note how many players, particularly poor ones, end their backswing with a fancy flourish. Some do it unconsciously. Some have the misguided notion that this makes them look more professional. Needless to say, it does not, but it does interfere with the smoothness of the forward swing. Nor should the backswing come to an abrupt halt and then reverse itself on exactly the same plane. Rather, at the end of the backswing, the racket head drops slightly before beginning forward so that it forms the arc of a small circle. This should be one, smooth, unbroken

e) Strings are still perpendicular to ground as racket makes contact with ball.

f) Body is facing net and racket continues to move forward after ball contact.

g) In follow through, racket winds up pointed directly at net, as in back view above.

If racket continues too far to left, follow-through is incorrect.

A common error is finishing forehand drive with racket over left shoulder.

motion. Your grip on the racket should be solid but not so tight that you squeeze the life out of it and your hand. Also check that your wrist is firm. If you collapse your wrist, this will cause the racket to wobble.

As your arm straightens and your body pivots in the forward motion, your racket head should be at hip height when its face is parallel to the net. The imaginary ball you are hitting will be ahead and to the right of your left, or anchor, foot. Your weight will already be on your left foot when you hit it, and the stroking motion will be slightly upwards to carry the ball over the net. Now continue your forward swing so that the racket moves on in an upward motion, finishing with the head at shoulder height and pointed upwards and directly towards the net.

The racket should not wind up point-ing off to the left, or over your left shoulder, or down around your waistline or somewhere near your left elbow. Nor should the face of the racket be angled up or down. At the end of the follow-through on the forehand drive, your racket should be pointing in the direction in which you hit the ball. If you hit it over your left shoulder, which is not easy to do, there would be some reason for the racket head winding up there. But if you hit it over the net, which is, after all, the object of the game, then that is the direction in which your racket should be aimed. Note the word. It is an accurate description of what you do with your racket in a proper forehand drive. You *aim* it in the direction in which you want the ball to travel.

With all this talk of hitting balls, you are by now impatient to get out and

Beginners who take too big a backswing are often late making contact with ball.

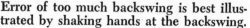

Error of too much backswing is best illustrated by shaking hands at the backswing.

actually hit some. I cannot overemphasize, however, exactly how important to developing a sound, smooth drive the time you spend in front of the mirror is. Tennis is a game of form, and you have one tremendous advantage in tackling the game as an adult over all those people who began playing it as children. You do not have a lifetime of bad habits to break. If you make good form an

integral part of your game from the moment you begin, the strokes you develop will be sound and consistent. Good strokes are built upon good form. Bad form will never produce better than patched-together, undependable strokes. This does not mean that you cannot play, and even play passably well, with poor form. (Just look around at your own club and note the broad

Improved backswing is achieved by taking racket straight back.

Again, this is illustrated by shaking hands at the backswing. Note more natural feel.

range of style on the courts.) But you will never achieve the full level of your potential. (Look around at your club again. Note how many people play at exactly the same level today as they did ten years ago. It is a safe bet that if they play for another fifty years, they will not improve their game because they have reached the limits of their potential. You, on the other hand, can improve

steadily with every game you play, indefinitely, if you begin with a sound, stroke-proof foundation.)

So spend a few extra minutes before the mirror. Run through the entire motion from the ready position through the follow-through. Do this not three or four times but a dozen times or more, until your movements are free-flowing, smooth and natural-feeling. Then try stopping the exercise at different points: at the end of the backswing; at the point of impact with the ball; at the end of the follow-through. Check visually the position of your racket, your driving arm; check your grip and the position of your hips, shoulders, head and feet. Has your wrist collapsed? Are you dropping the racket head at the end of the backswing? Is the racket face open, or closed, as you pivot forward? Are your hips and shoulders moving together? Are you moving the racket with the thrust of your whole body or just with your arm? Is your elbow comfortably bent as you move into the backswing? Is it almost straight on the forward swing? If you can master all these parts of the proper forehand-drive form now, before you ever actually hit a ball, you will be free to concentrate solely on the ball when you reach the court. The time you spend in front of the mirror now can mean the difference between playing good tennis later or remaining forever a duffer.

Let us assume then that you have perfected a smooth, flowing forehand drive before the mirror and are now ready for the real thing. A friend who can throw a ball so that it bounces in approximately the same spot nine out of ten times is essential at this stage. Since it is best to concentrate on hitting the ball with a proper stroke before you also tackle the footwork involved in getting to the ball, it makes sense not to have to chase them all over the court. So do not use your neighbor's six-year-old son or your arthritic Aunt Millie. You have enough handicaps as it is.

Stand just inside the base line in the center of the court with your pitching partner at the net on your side. This will put him far enough away from you to

Beginners often crowd ball, hitting it too close. Note cramped arm, square body.

Wrong way to hit a low ball. Again arm is cramped, body square and too erect.

Correct contact with ball is made by reaching for it, with arm extended, body sideways to net.

A firm wrist helps assure accuracy.

A collapsed wrist can spoil the stroke.

Putting it all together means putting the ball where you want it.

This stroke should be a winner.

give you time to judge the flight and bounce of the ball and still make a complete backswing before bringing the racket forward to the strike zone. This should all be one smooth motion, exactly as it was before the mirror.

You will hear a lot about the strike zone when you begin hitting balls. This is the area in which racket and ball make contact, and maintain contact for a given distance and span of time. Although one commonly speaks of *hitting* the ball in tennis, this is a convenient term rather than a technically accurate description of what actually happens when racket and ball meet. The word *hit* implies a glancing blow, a single brief contact that begins and ends in the same instant. Although the word is used in tennis regularly (and will continue to be used by me and just about everyone else who talks of tennis), what really happens is quite different. At the point of impact, the strings of the racket meet the rounded surface of the ball and compress it so that some 40 percent or more of the ball's rounded surface is flattened before it leaves the strings of the racket. In simpler terms, when the ball makes contact with the racket, it actually sinks into the strings and is carried forward this way. The racket and ball maintain this contact for a distance of perhaps a foot or more. This is what is meant by *stroking* the ball, or *hitting through* the ball. The strings of the racket hold and then move the ball. It is this stroking action that gives the ball direction, control and pace. This is why it is so important that the follow-through move forward along the path of the ball.

The area in which the racket and ball make contact and maintain contact is called the strike zone. In the forehand

The strike zone is slightly ahead and to the right of your anchor foot.

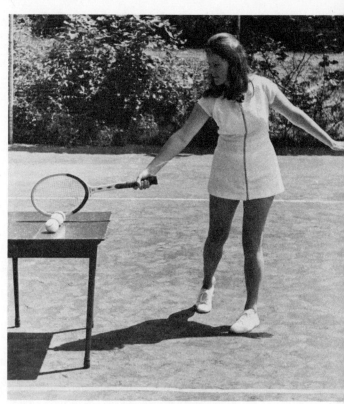

Welby Van Horn uses three balls on the ground to demonstrate strike zone.

Balls may also be placed on a **hip-height** table.

drive, this is slightly ahead and to the right of the left or anchor foot. Various professionals have various ways of illustrating the strike zone to a beginner. Welby Van Horn uses three tennis balls placed on the ground. The first is on a line with the toe of the left or anchor foot and about a racket's length to the right of the foot. The other two balls are lined up, about 6 inches apart, in front of the first ball. The racket when brought forward should travel over all three balls before continuing on into the follow-through. Some pros use a table of about hip height, or slightly lower, on which the three balls are placed in a row, much as Welby places them on the ground. In making the forehand stroke, the racket actually sweeps the balls from the table. Dennis Van der Meer

sometimes uses an unstrung racket and three or four balls skewered on a straight piece of wire. He holds the skewered ball in the strike zone, at hip height and parallel to the ground, while the beginner strokes the unstrung racket down the wire until all the balls have passed through it. The chief value of such an approach is to dramatically demonstrate exactly how long racket and ball are in contact during the stroke. The longer they are in contact, the more accurate the flight of the ball will be.

If the ball is carried on the racket strings properly through the entire strike zone, the follow-through will invariably wind up where it is supposed to. There is no way for the racket to end up over the left shoulder if it has remained with the ball for the full stroke, since it should then automatically follow the path of the ball off the strings and over the net.

That is the way the ball is supposed to be stroked. But what should be and what is, alas, are often worlds apart. The most common mistake of the beginner is to interrupt his forward swing just as the racket makes contact with the ball, or just before. Instead of stroking the ball, he swats it. Or he pokes it. Instead of the ball being carried through the strike zone on the strings, it is propelled off them like a missile . . . an unguided missile.

Anyone who watches club tennis long enough will inevitably spot the windmill player. He is the fellow whose forward swing is made entirely with his

In making forehand stroke, racket should sweep balls from table.

Beginners often hit the ball too far back with weight on the wrong foot.

Or they hit it too close to the body and off balance.

arm. He winds up, literally like a windmill, and then swings at the ball as if he were trying to shake his arm loose from the socket. He may give a small grunt as the racket slams into the ball. He almost certainly will give a groan as the ball bloops into the net or sails two courts away. This is also the fellow who usually develops some form of tennis elbow because he plays the entire game with his arm.

Then there is the court killer who attacks every ball as if it were a poisonous cobra about to strike at him. He smashes at the ball with manic vengeance, and occasionally sends it whizz-

ing like a bullet over the net for a winner. But most of the time its flight is as wild as his fury. The reason is that it is virtually impossible to aim a ball that has been struck a roundhouse blow. This kind of shot does take physical strength. And it does look impressive to the uninitiated. But since it invariably involves flicking the wrist and jerking the racket at the point of impact, control of the ball is sacrificed to speed. Winners who have this kind of shot are just lucky. The player who insists on blasting the ball is his own worst foe on the court.

So if you find yourself feeling your

Sometimes they act as if it will bite them.

Or as if they were using a shovel instead of a racket.

Wheaties and eager to demonstrate your strength, forget it. Remember instead to slow down, steady your stroke and aim the ball on the racket. Stop at the end of the stroke and check your follow-through. Hold the pose—arms, shoulders, hips and feet—exactly as you ended the stroke. Are you in the same position you saw in the mirror, or did you let it all fall apart when you actually put a ball into the act? To many beginners, the presence of the ball does make a difference. They can execute the forehand drive beautifully in the mirror, but once the ball has been added, the formerly free-flowing movement of

the stroke deteriorates into a series of jerks. As discouraging as this may seem, and believe me I have been through the discouragement, it happens to most beginners some time or another. The perpetual duffer shrugs his shoulders and continues to jerk at the ball. The more serious student forgets the ball for a while and goes back to grooving his swing without the ball. Do this whenever you find yourself having trouble with your stroke. It will pay off in points later.

You will not need anyone to tell you when you finally stroke the ball properly. Not only will it go where you want it to, but the stroke will *feel* good. Feel is one of the most difficult elements to define, as well as to teach, in tennis. To some extent, it is an innate sense that varies from individual to individual, just as ESP does. It is doubtless tied as well to one's coordination, timing and ability to concentrate. But on the more tangible side, it is an element you can hear and detect through your racket and arm. There is a definite difference between the sound of a ball hitting the outside of the strings, near the edge of the racket face, and the sound of one hitting squarely in the center of the strings. The latter sound is deep, resounding. To stretch the imagination a bit, it is comparable to the melodious echo one might hear when shouting down a well, whereas the sound of a ball struck on the edge of the strings is

flat and sharp, as one's echo would be off a cement wall. Even more distinctive is the sound of the ball hit off the wood or metal frame of the racket, or off its handle. You cannot miss the metallic ring of a rim shot. It usually heralds a ball sent soaring straight up into the sky or off over the nearest fence. There is only one more disconcerting sound, and that is only possible with a metal racket. It is the flat and abrupt *thrup* as the ball comes to a sudden stop compressed into the open throat of the racket. It is hard to feel more foolish on the court, especially if you spend the first minute looking around for the ball.

But when the ball resounds cleanly off the center of the strings—the sweet spot, it is called—there is no mistaking the sound. And unless you are totally insensitive, there is also no mistaking

These photographs illustrate the dramatic difference between poor (left) and proper (right) weight distribution and balance.

Collapsed wrist, square body position and poor balance automatically doom this shot.

the solid, satisfying feel of the stroke through your racket and up your arm. Behind a properly stroked ball is a combination of balance, timing and the marshaling of your entire body. You will have pivoted smoothly into the shot, with all your weight directed behind it, and your follow-through aimed directly after the ball. By mastering these basic fundamentals even the most delicate hothouse flower can develop an accurate, powerful forehand drive without exhausting her resources.

Backhand Drives

No beginner ever believes it, and many refuse even to consider it, but the backhand drive is a more natural stroke than the forehand. Impossible, you say! Not if you analyze the basic differences between the forehand and the backhand. In the forehand drive, your racket arm is the farther one from the ball and the net, and your body is between your racket and the ball as you prepare for the shot. As you pivot forward and stroke the ball, your racket must come partway across your body in the follow-through. Now look at the backhand. Your racket arm is the one nearer the ball and the net. Your body presents no interference between racket arm and ball. Your stroke as you pivot forward is out and away from the body. There is clearly greater freedom to the swing.

If this explanation has not convinced you—and although it is all quite logical and true, it rarely convinces the novice when he first tackles the backhand—try a more simple illustration. Take a penny and toss it at a point on the floor in front of you. The odds are that you tossed it with a backhand motion. Have you ever tossed rings at the necks of bottles at a county fair or amusement park? Have you ever pitched horseshoes? How do you deal a deck of cards? The way you do all these things, if you are like most people, is backhanded. The reason you do them backhanded is because that motion is the more natural one. Even politicians toss their hats into the ring backhanded. But for some reason which has never been adequately analyzed, beginners in tennis are more leery of the backhand stroke than of any other. Before they ever try it, they convince themselves that they will be unable to do it.

This may be one reason it is often a problem stroke for the novice. Another reason is doubtless that right-handed people are more or less "right-sided" and tend to feel more comfortable moving to the right than to the left. Also, in most other backhanded activities, the elbow is kept relatively close to the body. It is in tennis too—on the backswing—but in the stroke forward, the arm is extended and straightened, which may feel unnatural to the novice at first. All it requires is a little practice to make it feel as comfortable as last year's girdle.

Besides, there is one really important fact about the backhand that every beginner should know and remind himself of regularly. Although it may take a little longer to learn and to feel at ease with than the forehand, once learned, the backhand drive is the most dependable of all strokes. It can also be the most powerful, because you lean into it a little farther than you do into the forehand and thus put more of your weight behind the stroke. Moreover, it is the

least likely to desert you in those frustrating slumps all tennis players experience at one time or another when they are "off" their game. For some inexplicable reason, although one's forehand may crumble, one's service may tumble and one's volley may disintegrate into the clay, one's backhand will invariably remain true and reliable. And if that is not enough to convince you to make a real effort on this stroke, there is yet another reason: when the backhand is properly made, there is no shot in tennis that feels quite as good. The satisfaction of returning a perfect backhand low over the net and deep into the opposite corner is enormous. For a beginner, it is a genuine thrill.

Balance is the key to the backhand as it is to the forehand. Again, the best place to work on this stroke is in front of the mirror. In the ready position, shift the racket and your grip to the Eastern backhand. Turn your body to the left and sideways to the mirror as you did for the backhand balance exercise. As you do, bring your racket back with both hands. Your left hand should cradle the throat, as in the ready position, supporting it firmly but loosely. Your right elbow should be bent and the arm close but not cramped across your chest. As you learned in the original backhand-balance exercise, your shoulders and hips will be turned away from the mirror slightly more than in the forehand position, which means you will take the racket head back a bit farther than you did for the forehand.

Throughout the backswing, the face of the racket should remain perpendicular to the floor. At the end of the backswing, the racket should be angled slightly upward, but not so much that it looks like a lollipop on a stick. A good

Backhand Drive: a) Grip has been shifted to backhand as racket begins backswing.

c) Eyes remain on ball as backswing is completed.

b) Left hand guides racket head back as body is turned sideways to net.

d) Weight transfer onto anchor foot is completed before racket makes contact with ball.

e) Ball is hit out and in front with straight arm and full thrust of body.

f) Forward hip and shoulder are lower in backhand drive than in forehand.

g) Weight remains on anchor foot to completion of follow-through.

way to judge the proper angle is to check in the mirror that you can see the circular butt end of the racket beneath your right hand. If you cannot, the racket head is too high.

The end of the backhand backswing, like the end of that for the forehand, is not an abrupt halt but rather a small, circular motion in which the racket head drops slightly, describing an arc, before beginning the forward swing. Again, it is not a flourish or a grand gesture. As you then move the racket forward, your weight should shift squarely onto the right foot so that the weight transfer is completed *before* the racket makes contact with the ball. As in the forehand drive, the strike zone begins about a racket's length to the side and forward of the toes of the anchor foot.

The ball is hit out and in front of you with an almost straight arm and the full thrust of your body behind it. Remember that you lean deeper into the backhand drive than into the forehand, which is why your forward hip and shoulder will be lower in this stroke than in the other. As the racket passes through the strike zone, it continues with a slight upward motion towards the net. If you have followed through properly, your weight should remain on the right foot, your shoulders and hips should be square to the net and your racket should be pointed directly at the net with the face perpendicular to the floor and the head angled upward.

Practice this several times before the mirror until your motions from ready position to follow-through are fluid and relaxed. Once you smooth out this

Backhand Drive From Rear: a) Racket head is angled upward at end of backswing.

b) Body pivots on rear foot as weight is transferred forward.

c) Hips and shoulders are square to net at end of follow-through.

A friend can help you get the feeling of leaning into the backhand.

Common error in backswing is pointing racket head too high.

A ball hit with racket too open is aimed towards heaven.

One hit with racket too closed is destined for the net.

stroke, you should begin to feel the greater sense of freedom it gives you. If you do not, follow your motions more closely in the mirror. You are undoubtedly doing something wrong. Check your backswing, your feet, body position and racket handling. Swing through the stroke a half-dozen times, watching carefully in the mirror. Once you have smoothed out the rough spots, you

should feel distinctly more at ease and graceful with this stroke than with the forehand.

Now take what you have learned in the mirror to the court and make sure you work with someone who can bounce a ball to you with reasonable accuracy. Concentrate on keeping your swing as smooth and free-flowing as it was in front of the mirror. Try to stroke the ball

Another backhand error is leading with the elbow and hitting the ball too far back.

Here the weight is on the wrong foot. The arm is cramped and the ball is being hit too low and too far back.

Reaching behind for a backhand invariably throws one off balance.

well out in front of you, keeping it on the center of the strings as long as possible and following through towards the net with your racket. Everything that was said earlier about the forehand applies to the backhand, but there are a few pitfalls that occur more commonly with the backhand.

Because he has to change grips, the beginner is sometimes slower getting into position and making his backswing. This in turn makes him late bringing the racket forward, which means it meets the ball behind him instead of in front of him. With his weight back on his adjustment foot, instead of on his anchor foot, he must hit the shot with his arm alone since he cannot put the thrust of his body into the stroke. Besides reducing power, this generally produces an incomplete or sloppy follow-through and a ball that goes up and out of the court. Beginners also frequently collapse their wrists on the backhand, a fault which also is linked to hitting the ball too far behind the strike zone.

Another common error is hitting the ball too close to the body. This cramps the arm and elbow, preventing a smooth forward stroke and often results in the elbow leading the racket head. The lever in the backhand stroke is centered in the muscles in the back and shoulder. By leading with the elbow, the shoulder and upper arm muscles become virtually useless. Women have this problem more frequently than men, presumably because their shoulder and arm muscles are weaker. One way to compensate for this weakness is to practice at first with a two-handed backhand. For many years, in spite of such two-fisted luminaries as Pancho Segura, Cliff Drysdale and Chris Evert, the two-handed backhand was frowned up-

A good two-handed backswing.

Both hands on the racket provide extra strength.

on by most professionals because it limited the reach of the player. Its advantage with a weak player, however, is that it provides extra strength to execute the full stroke while preventing the elbow from getting ahead of the racket.

With both hands on the racket, the hips and shoulders are forced to pivot forward for the stroke. As in a conventional backhand, at the end of the follow-through the racket head should be at about shoulder level and pointed directly towards the net. After the backhand is mastered with the two-handed

Some players follow through with two hands.

Others drop the left hand after hitting ball.

stroke, it is relatively easy to drop the left hand and to hit a smooth, free-flowing one-handed drive.

If you are conscious of the pitfalls peculiar to the backhand, and watch for them, stopping as soon as you begin blooping balls into the net or out over the fence, to analyze why; and if you concentrate on your form and the smoothness of your stroke, even if you miss the ball altogether at first, you will eventually develop a backhand that will bring you pleasure and points for as long as you play tennis.

X. The Drop-shot, Half-volley and Lob

You now have the two basic ground strokes in tennis. The only other one you should consider incorporating into your game as a beginner and intermediate player is the lob. The drop-shot and the half-volley are best left to considerably more experienced and skilled players. They are discussed here only so that you will know what they are when you see them used on court or hear people talk about them.

A deliberate drop-shot is well beyond the ability of most elementary players. Even in advanced and tournament play, it is a shot that is used sparingly. The drop-shot is also called a dink-shot, a chip, a chop, a slice, a nothing-ball and a no-no because, depending upon the kind of spin put on the ball, it drops low into your opponent's court, usually just over the net, and then bounces backwards or sideways or barely comes up at all. The ball is hit with considerable wrist action—which leaves the beginner out right off—either with the forehand or the backhand. Ideally the initial approach is disguised as if for a normal drive since the greatest asset of this shot is its element of surprise. If one's opponent mistakes it initially for a normal drive, he will be caught sleeping on the base line. Even if he recognizes it instantly, he will need the speed of a track star to reach the net from the base line before the ball collapses. It is thus most effective on tired, clumsy, elderly, dim-witted, left-footed and myopic opponents. Obviously it loses its effectiveness if used too often. The overzealous drop-shooter will find himself losing opponents as well, since most players, particularly good ones who enjoy hard, fast balls, despise and detest bloopers.

The beginner's blooper, which is rarely intentional, differs from the deliberate drop-shot although the results are similar: a virtually lifeless ball that collapses just over the net. Behind the beginner's "drop-shot" is a miss-hit, but like deliberate drop-shots, his bloopers can drive an opponent crazy. Even if they win points, which they often do, they will not win friends on the courts.

Like the drop-shot, the half-volley is neither a beginner's nor an intermediate's stroke since it is simply too difficult. As noted earlier, it is not a true volley since the ball does bounce before being hit, but it is hit, either forehand or backhand, only inches from the

The difficult half-volley. Note balance and reach.

in order to volley it before the bounce, he should certainly do so.

For all but advanced players, the half-volley is a desperation shot, taken usually because a player has found himself caught in the no-man's-land midway between net and base line with the ball headed straight for his ankles. Or he may be standing flat-footed at the back of the court when a deep drive to the tape catches him unawares. In either case, it is probably a lost point because the only way to get the ball back under such circumstances is the half-volley, and the odds against a beginner's executing it successfully are overwhelming.

The half-volley requires split-second reflexes, great flexibility in knees and body, perfect timing and absolute concentration on the ball as it meets the racket. The great Bill Tilden refused to coach either the drop-shot or the half-volley because he believed that no player should monkey with either until he was an absolute master of all other strokes. And when a player was that good, Tilden said, he was then good enough to evolve his own way of playing these strokes since they are basically a matter of "feel" or tennis instinct.

Which brings us to the lob—another case entirely. This is perhaps the most frequently overlooked and grossly underestimated of the ground shots, yet it is one that a beginner cannot only master with little difficulty but also use to great advantage from his earliest games on. It is an invaluable asset when you find yourself, as doubtless you often will in beginning play, pulled way out of position on one shot with no hope of getting back into position in time to return the next. You can buy time with a lob, which is nothing more than a forehand

ground. If it is hit two feet above the ground or higher, it is no longer a half-volley but becomes a conventional drive. Thus the only difference between a drive and a half-volley is the height at which the ball is hit, but that difference is significant indeed.

Considering that the half-volley, or pick-up, as it is often called, is one of the most difficult strokes in tennis, why would anyone choose such a shot over a drive? The answer, of course, is that in most cases he has no choice. When a ball bounces right at his feet, or even inches behind his heels, this is the only possible way to return it. If he has an opportunity either to run far enough behind the ball to permit it to rise before hitting it, or to move in closer to the net or backhand drive hit with the racket face open, or angled slightly upward, so that you send the ball soaring high into the sky, hoping it comes down again in your opponent's court. While he scrambles after it, and then awaits its descent, you can be scrambling back into ready position for his return . . . *if* he returns it.

When the lob is used in this manner, it is called a defensive lob. There are two other kinds of lobs: the offensive and the outrageous. Most beginning and intermediate play is defensive, as it should be, since the principal object of the beginner's game is to get the ball back over the net in the hope that his opponent will make the error on its return. But the lob is a stroke that can be used offensively from the beginning.

One of the beauties of the lob is that it often so flusters or frustrates your opponent that he flubs its return. The reason is principally timing. Because the ball is in flight so much longer than in an ordinary drive or volley, the player has more than ample time to get into position to hit it—in fact, he has so much time it can throw off his judgment, stroke and balance. He may swing too soon, or not soon enough. He may punch at the ball instead of stroking through as he should. At the last minute, misled by the deceptive slowness of the ball's descent, he may decide to volley it before it bounces. This, for anybody but an experienced player, is almost always a disaster.

Two other common errors in returning a lob are hitting the ball too close to the ground, as if it were a half-volley, or letting it bounce too high. In both cases, the player has misjudged the point of the ball's bounce—in the first, by getting in position too close to

it; in the second, too far behind it. Ideally, a high lob should be hit *after* the bounce, when the ball is at hip height, exactly as one would hit a normal forehand or backhand drive. Some players become so hypnotized by the descent of a very high lob that they watch it transfixed, as if rooted to the court in a position from which return is impossible. You cannot take your eyes off a lobbed ball for a single instant but you cannot station yourself in one spot waiting for it either. You must keep your eyes on the ball and your feet moving at all times so that you are flexible enough to get into position even if the ball lands in an unexpected spot.

Another beauty of the shot is that even experienced players have a terrible time returning a high lob that bounces deep into their backhand corner. Returning such a ball requires running way out behind the base line. A backhand shot from this position is extremely difficult to make, and even if returned, if often falls short into your court where you can put it away before your opponent has even gotten back to his base line.

Although you are not likely in the early stages of play to come up against too many singles players who rush to net, should you, the lob over your opponent's head is an almost certain winner. In doubles, where one or both of your opponents will be at net most of the time, it is a marvelously effective way of putting the ball out of reach of their rackets. Another advantage of the lob is that it changes the pace of a game, which often puts your opponent off balance.

The outrageous lob is an offensive lob with a twist—figuratively, not literally. It usually drives your opponent up the nearest fence. When the sun is high over the court, a lob that makes your opponent look directly up into it in order to follow the ball is almost certain to give him sunspots, to ruin his return and to outrage him. A lob into wind blowing from your opponent's court to yours is also outrageous because the ball will appear to be coming down in one spot but will actually bounce in another. A lob that goes up so high that it takes forever to come down can do outrageous things to your opponent's timing. All are legitimate and effective point getters, although if you use them too often they are certain to make outrageous inroads into the number of people willing to play with you.

The key to good lobbing is to fit it into the pattern of the game. Look around your club again. You will doubtless note that most of the players fall into one of two categories: those who lob all the time, and those who never lob. The best players fall somewhere in between. They use the lob as a regular part of their game, offensively and defensively, not just in situations where it is the most logical shot but at unexpected times to throw off the pace and balance of the opposition.

The only real difference between forehand and backhand lobs and drives is that in the lob, the racket face is opened slightly and the racket lifts the ball up higher than in a drive. The backswing is exactly the same. This is important not only to the production of the stroke but also to the surprise element of the shot. Your opponent should be unaware that you are going to lob until your racket is actually on the ball. You still must stroke through it, but you lift as you hit the ball. Your follow-through is as essential to the lob as it is

to the drive. It should be smooth and uninterrupted. At its end, your racket will be pointed higher as it follows the path of the ball upwards. It is more difficult to aim a lob than a drive, but just as with the other ground strokes, the longer the ball stays on the strings of the racket, the more controlled its flight will be.

This stroke, too, has its pitfalls. The three most common are: the ball may sail beyond the base line; it may bloop over your opponent's head within reach of his racket; it may drop too close to the net. The first situation is a certain lost point. There are no home runs in tennis. The second is a 99 percent loser, unless your partner is totally incompetent, since it is a perfect setup for an unreturnable smash. The third is almost as likely a loser since it can be angled just over the net to either side of your court with little hope of your reaching it.

The best way to avoid all three errors is practice. The lob is a shot you have to hit over and over again until you get the feel of it. This applies as well to returning lobs. The more you practice, the more your judgment and timing will improve. The two-court exercise Will Sherwood practiced with me when I first began to play at Gipsy Trail was invaluable training in the lob, and has paid off in points in the years since.

A point to remember when lobbing is that a cross-court lob is not only harder for your opponent to return but, because there is more court for it to cover, it also gives you a greater margin of safety against hitting the ball out. The harder you hit a lob, the more steeply you must angle it upwards to prevent its going out. Only practice will teach you the right touch in this stroke.

Experiment with all kinds of high, low and intermediate lobs to get the feel of what you can make the ball do. Concentrate on trying to get your lob just high enough to clear your opponent's upflung racket on a jump, but not so high that the ball gets lost in the clouds. A medium-high lob over his head comes down faster, giving your opponent less time to run back and get into position to return it.

At the risk of being repetitious: This is a stroke that can only be perfected with practice, but it is well worth the effort. A good lob is a versatile and invaluable asset in any player's arsenal.

XI. The Volley

Sooner or later, as I found almost immediately upon returning from Puerto Rico, you will have to abandon the security of the base line for the insecurity of the net. If you play singles, you can postpone this dreaded moment practically indefinitely. But if you play doubles, it is a traumatic experience you cannot avoid. And regardless of what the professionals and other books say, it *is* a traumatic experience for a beginner. Every ball seems aimed directly at his tonsils—many actually are, since a rank novice at net is a pigeon for the opposition. I spent most of my first games at net ducking, flinching, closing my eyes, sidestepping, throwing up my hands to protect my teeth, using the racket as a shield and fending off balls with my fists. The sense of being totally vulnerable, and utterly ineffectual, was all-prevailing. It was also quite natural.

A tennis ball looks entirely different at net than it does from the backcourt. (If it does not to you, you probably should not be reading this book. Go play in a tournament somewhere.) The ball at net is faster, closer and decidedly more menacing. There is no time for the long, fluid backswing and the graceful follow-

through you have devoted so much effort and hours to acquiring. While you are thinking about form, the ball is whizzing by your ear like a rocket. But as threatening and hopeless as the situation at net may seem, good net strokes are considerably easier to master than good ground strokes.

To begin with, the basic ones—the forehand and backhand volleys—are much less complex. There are also drop volleys and lob volleys, but like drop-shots and half-volleys, they are well beyond the capabilities, and therefore the aspirations, of a beginner. Few weekend players, even those at top level, can execute either with consistency. But just so you recognize what is happening should you ever see them in play, the ball that is drop-volleyed, either forehand or backhand, barely skims the net and then drops . . . dead. Literally. It is virtually impossible to return, but since it requires such a deft touch and so much backspin, you might as well forget trying to learn it. At least for a decade or two. The same applies to the lob volley, which is just that: a volley that is returned with a lob. Since this too requires an extremely delicate touch and precise timing, it is best left to the big boys.

The backhand and forehand volleys are another story. They are shots that every beginner should include in his repertoire as soon as his ground strokes are under control. Learn the ground strokes first. You will need them first. But once they are under your belt, do not postpone acquiring the volley. It will serve you well and make you friends.

Since a volley is any ball that is hit in flight before it bounces, volleys can be made from almost any position in the court. Most are made somewhere between the service line and the net. A rule of thumb is to stand back from the net just far enough to be able to touch it with the end of your outstretched racket. The only difference between your ready position at net and that on the base line is in your knees. They should be flexed a little more for the volley so that you are in a modified crouch. The advantage of this position is that it brings your eyes down to a lower level so that you can better follow the flight of the ball. But a modified crouch does not mean that you should be stooped over like an elderly ragpicker poking into a garbage bin. Your body should be upright and your weight on the balls of your feet. At no time, especially at net, should you be caught flat-footed. If your heels are on the ground, and your knees are stiff, you greatly reduce your ability to move quickly into a new position for a shot.

The volley itself is a ministroke. There is no backswing and no real follow-through, as we have learned it to this point. The actual contact of racket on ball is sudden, hard and without the refinements of swinging through the strike zone one needs with a ground stroke. The volley is to the drive what a peasant is to an aristocrat. But it does its own particular job best, just as a peasant may do best with a shovel and an aristocrat with a pen. Although the volley and the drive, technically, are both strokes, the volley is a punch and the drive is a caress. Each has its value and its place.

You do not need a backswing in a volley because the oncoming ball creates sufficient force for its own return. As the ball approaches, rather than bringing the racket back in order to swing it forward, use it instead as a blocking power. As the ball approaches, you *thrust* your racket at it, actually pushing it back over the net. This is a quick, sharp, stabbing motion, exactly the kind you would use swatting a fly with a magazine. It is not a jerk or a wrist flick. Your wrist, in fact, should be locked and firm throughout the volley, and your grip on the racket should be absolutely solid. It is especially important to remind yourself to squeeze just as you block the ball, otherwise the force of the oncoming ball will easily twist the racket in your hand.

Just as in a ground stroke, the racket must meet the ball ahead of you in a volley. Various professionals have various theories on how to grip the racket at net. Some suggest using conventional forehand and backhand grips, depending upon whether the volley is forehand or backhand. Others recommend a backhand grip for both. Still others prefer a single grip midway between the forehand and the backhand for both strokes. Almost every professional agrees that the ball should be hit on opposite sides of the racket face for the forehand and backhand volley, exactly as with the ground strokes, regardless of the grip used.

My personal preference for players of modest talent and ability is a single grip, the modified Eastern, which falls somewhere between the forehand and the backhand. The reason is simple. Most adult beginners question the speed of their own reactions at net. The ball always seems to be coming faster than they believe they can handle it and they are convinced they cannot get the racket on it soon enough. This is not necessarily true. In most cases, it is not true at all. But changing initial impressions is comparable to changing grips. It takes a certain amount of time. If the beginner does not have to worry about changing from a forehand to a backhand grip, he can concentrate sooner on punching the ball back into the opponent's court. And since the volley *is* a punch, involving less finesse in its basic forms than a ground stroke, the modified Eastern grip is more than adequate to handle both forehand and backhand volleys.

The real keys to an effective volley are your eyes and your feet. The eyes come first. If you take them off the ball for the briefest instant, forget about the point. You cannot expect to make your racket connect with the ball if you are not looking at it . . . constantly. This sounds logical enough, but when the ball comes whizzing towards him, the beginner almost instinctively blinks. It is a natural reflex. It also only takes one blink to lose the ball. Even more advanced players have a strong tendency to momentarily take their eyes off the ball. This is understandable when it crosses the net like a bullet. But it also happens when the ball bloops over the net like a marshmallow. Marshmallows

at net, especially in club play, are as common as bullets, and are just as easily missed. Nine out of ten times the reason for missing is looking away from the ball at the moment it should be struck.

The best and probably only way to correct this is to practice hitting balls at net, deliberately reminding yourself with each to watch the ball. You will be surprised at how useful it is to make a habit of saying to yourself "watch the ball" or "eyes on the ball" each time a ball comes over the net. The importance of keeping your eye on the ball, not just in volleying but in every stroke, is so great that it is discussed at more length in Chapter XIV.

In addition to your eyes, your feet are a major factor in volleying. In order to hit the ball ahead of you, you must step forward towards it. It is the full thrust of your body that puts the punch in a volley, not a disembodied poke of your racket. On a forehand volley of a ball that comes to your right side, your *left* foot steps forward and to the right so that at the point of contact between racket and ball, your left shoulder has turned towards the net and both you and your racket are moving forward. On a backhand volley, it is your *right* foot that steps across your left, and forward, and your right shoulder that turns to the net so that the thrust of your body and racket is towards the net at the point of impact.

Again, your own club is probably the best place to look for horrible examples of how not to volley. Study a few of your fellow members at net and note how many of them back off or away from a volley before hitting it, *if* they hit it. Note especially how many of them take a backswing with their racket in doing so. This backswing is what forces them to back off in order to reach the ball. The instants they lose in taking the racket back and then reversing its motion are enough to permit the ball to get by them. If they then hit the ball at all, they hit it late, which means that it is probably hit out of control. Think of the volley as an *interception* shot which must be taken well before it reaches you. You cannot wait for it to get where you are standing. You must surge forward, intercepting its path, and punch it back while you are still

able to aim and control it. This is done simply by angling your racket face towards the direction in which you want the ball to go. If you are moving aggressively towards the ball, its impact upon your racket will take care of the rest.

Besides hitting behind the ball and late, beginners also run into a lot of wrist problems in their volleys. The volley is hit with a stiff wrist. If you think of the volley as being comparable in many ways to the jab of a prizefighter, you will understand how important it is to keep the wrist immobile. Make a fist of

A good forehand volley. Note body position, weight on left foot, left shoulder towards net.

Good backhand volley position—ready to punch ball back.
Note weight on right foot, right shoulder towards net.

Good backhand volley position after punching ball (player
has extended thumb for added strength). Note little
or no follow through.

one hand and punch the palm of your other hand with it. Note how stiff the wrist remains. To be effective, it cannot bend. This is equally true in the volley. Beginners most often run into trouble when they attempt to make a backhand volley by turning their rackets and hitting the ball on the same face used in a forehand volley. It is virtually impossible to keep a stiff wrist if the backhand volley is made this way.

It is also virtually impossible to make a good return with this racket position. Many beginners are not even aware that they have used it, especially when the backhand volley is made close to the body or high. This is why it is important in the early stages of volleying to analyze exactly what you are doing with the racket. Check that you are not turning it upside down or forehand-side forward. One trick that often helps a novice is to keep the left hand on the racket throat throughout the backhand punch. This not only increases the strength behind the stroke but also ensures that it will be made from the proper backhand position. If you keep your hand on the throat, you cannot turn the racket around in making the shot. Another trick is to make a fist of the left hand and keep it directly behind the strings of the racket during the return. This exaggerates the sense of punching with the racket and again ensures that the proper side of the racket is used.

Another pitfall for beginners is hitting down on the ball instead of forward. The next time you watch an average game (this does not apply to Forest Hills or Wimbledon play), observe how many seemingly easy volleys are hit into the net. Looking away from the ball at the moment of truth is a leading

Common beginner's error: Racket face is turned to wrong side, wrist is collapsed.

Incorrect backhand volley position. Note collapsed wrist.

One aid to proper backhand volley is to hold throat of racket with left hand, to prevent turning it to wrong side.

Another is to hold left fist behind racket during return.

Good backhand volley. Note weight, balance, firm wrist.

Correct backhand position for a high volley.

Incorrect return of low volley. Body is square and stooping.

Exaggeration of correct way to return low volley. Practice by getting down on one knee to get under ball.

cause, but so is hitting down on the ball. If you and your racket are moving forward *towards* the ball, this is not likely to happen. Instead you will punch the ball forward, not down, when it makes contact with your racket, and rather than hitting it into the net, you will put it over. The exception, of course, is when the ball is already lower than the tape at the top of the net; punching it forward will put it into the net instead of over. The obvious rule is to attempt to return every volley before it has time to drop beneath the net.

It is always desirable to return a volley while the ball is still moving up; avoid letting the ball drop below the net. But sometimes this is unavoidable. Some balls are already coming down as

they cross the net. These are tough, particularly when they are also very close to the net. If you try to volley at exactly the moment the ball crosses the net on its downard path, your racket may hit the net and you will lose the point. If you are premature and try to return the ball before it has actually crossed the net, your shot will also be disqualified. The way to hit such a ball is to drop below the net along with it and, still using no backswing but with the racket face slightly open, to punch the ball back up and over the net. You cannot make this shot with stiff knees. Nor can you make it by reaching down from an erect body. You must get your entire body down low, bending your knees almost to the ground, or as low as is necessary to bring your hips down to ball height, and then punch the ball back up. If you attempt to return this low ball from an upright position, it will be scooped or shoveled into the net.

There is a simple exercise to develop the feel of getting down for a low volley that can be of great help to a beginner in learning to handle this difficult shot. With your body turned to the net for a forehand volley, actually drop down so that you are kneeling on your right knee with the weight and thrust of your body on your left foot. For greater balance, you can support yourself with your left hand on your left knee. Now have someone on the other side of the net throw balls directly to your racket head. Note how solidly they can be returned from this seemingly impossible position; note particularly the control you have. After you have returned a few dozen forehands, reverse the position and do the same thing with the backhand volley. Once you have the feel of this shot, stand up and practice quickly dropping to one knee or the other to return tossed volleys. As your sense of touch and balance on the low volley develops, you can slowly reduce the exaggeration of the deep kneebend until you are bending just low enough to return the ball back over the net.

Another exercise of value in developing a good volley is to practice volleying either on a backboard, if you are already reasonably proficient, or with another player, which is not as fast as the backboard and therefore somewhat easier for a beginner. You only need half a court for this exercise and your partner need not be an expert. Stand on either side of the net, about 8 to 10 feet from it, and volley the ball gently. Don't try to put it away; just try to keep it in play.

You will be surprised at how long you can keep a ball airborne if you concentrate. Obviously you must keep your eyes on it every instant. This means you cannot look at your partner. The moment the ball leaves his strings, you should be ready for it to meet yours. This exercise develops both your concentration and your reflexes. It is also an excellent antiflinching device. Flinching is one of the novice's greatest foes.

In one of the Mixed Doubles tournaments I played in at Gipsy Trail, I came up against a man who boasted loudly at the bar the weekend before the match that he was going to smash every volley directly at my teeth. So warned, I became armed. That week I took three one-hour lessons during which the club pro, overcoming his initial trepidations at the prospect of wiping out one of his best customers, directed every volley at my teeth. At first his volleys were deliberately slow and easy, but by the second hour he was convinced that I really wanted him to give me the business, and he did. He scored a direct hit only once but the fat lip was well worth the sense of confidence I developed at net by being prepared to meet a mouth-shot head-on. When the match took place, my opponent, true to his word, hit every ball to my incisors, and I returned just about everyone of them to his court, most of the time for points. Two-thirds of the way through, his partner was warning him through her own clenched teeth not to hit to the net man, and by the time we finally won the match, she was sending him looks that would sink ships.

Hitting to the net man is not always a losing game, but it can be a tricky one. The danger is that if he has any competence at all, he will return your ball

The hip ball—a difficult volley to return— is virtually impossible on forehand.

The best chance of returning a hip ball is with a backhand volley.

for a winner. The head-on mouth-shot, which looks so formidable and which my opponent used so unsuccessfully, is actually an easy shot to return if you are not afraid of it. You merely hold up the racket and block the ball back.

The most difficult shot looks considerably less formidable. This is the one that comes directly at your feet or at your hip. It is almost impossible to

jockey your racket and body into position to return it. But controlling its return to make it a winner rather than a sitting duck is equally difficult. As a beginner and intermediate, you would be wiser to concentrate on returning the volley away from the net man and into a part of the court that your opponent or opponents cannot reach. Leave the trick shots to the Wimbledon crowd.

XII. The Serve

More points are lost, more tempers are tried and more energy is wasted on the serve in club-level tennis than on any other stroke. Without question it is the most abused, misunderstood and undeveloped element of the average club game. There is absolutely no reason why it should be. The serve is the one stroke in tennis—the only one—that you control 100 percent. In every other stroke, the point at which you hit the ball is virtually determined by factors outside your control. You must first anticipate how fast the ball is traveling and where it is going to bounce, and then run to it and get into position before you can make your stroke. In the serve, you are already in position and it is you who determines the speed of the ball and the point at which it is to be hit.

Why, then, is the serve such a bugaboo to weekend players? The answer may surprise you. It is simply that most weekend players never make a genuine effort to understand the principles of the serve and then to put them into practice. Club players who each season devote hours with the pro to their forehands and backhands, who work tirelessly on their volleys, are notoriously negligent of their serves. The top pros never are. They understand the vital importance of service to their game and are forever grooving, honing and perfecting their serves. You will find them several times a week, if not every day, serving baskets of several hundred balls to an empty court. How many times have you seen your fellow club members take out a basket and do the same? And it is a safe bet that they need the practice considerably more than the pros.

Some years ago, when Billie Jean King was ranked among the top ten women players in the United States but before she had achieved the ultimate pinnacle in her sport, she was troubled by a serve she felt had not reached its full potential. By top tournament standards it was more than good enough when coupled with her other strokes to keep her in the forefront of competition for a long time to come. But this was not good enough for Billie Jean. She went to Australia and enlisted the aid of the great Harry Hopman, who took her serve apart and put it together again in a form quite different from its original. Where Billie Jean had been walking through most competition with her old serve, she now began losing to players of considerably less talent. And she lost consistently over a period of several months while she worked to perfect her new and potentially better serve. A lesser sportsman might have given up in disgust after the first week of defeats. Billie Jean has never been called a lesser sportsman. She stuck it out. At the end of what was perhaps the most grueling and discouraging period of her career, she emerged with a serve that put the final fine edge on an already superb game. With her new serve, she was no longer simply one of the top ten. She was now Queen of Tennis.

This is fine for a Billie Jean King, you say, who after all makes her living out of tennis. The average weekend player has neither the time nor the inclination to put that kind of effort into the game. That is true. But, then, the average weekend player, alas, puts no *sensible* effort into the game. He runs around on the court, he sweats, he gets a good workout, he has fun, but usually he stopped making a genuine effort to improve his game long ago. He is content to get by with an adequate game when with very little effort he could upgrade his game considerably. This applies to just about every level of weekend player, from the rankest beginner to the top-seeded player.

The characteristic weekend player will coast along with a static game rather than grow and improve. There are two mains reasons for this: lack of challenge and laziness. In tournament play, the player at the top is always being attacked from below. New faces and new talents are forever chipping away at his throne. No champion sits easily upon it. In club play, where the turn-

over in faces and talent is low, players fall into their particular niches and tend to remain there. Because they are not subjected to the constant challenges faced by tournament players, they are able to get by with a game that never grows.

The other reason, laziness, is obvious. The only time the majority of club players spend on the courts is in playing games. If they have a tennis date at 9, they arrive at 9, rally for perhaps five or ten minutes, and then immediately start the game. Rarely does a club player come out a half-hour or an hour early and work on the backboard or practice his serve. Even more rarely does he forego a game entirely in order to practice. Yet even a single hour each weekend devoted to reviewing and improving his strokes and serve could move him from one level to the next in a single season.

You do not have to go to Australia, you do not have to vanish into a tennis camp for an extended period, you do not have to put a top professional on retainer in order to upgrade your game. Certainly if you can and want to try any of these things, by all means do so. But the point is that you do not have to devote an inordinate amount of time, money and energy to improving your game. You can make it grow—consistently and steadily and almost indefinitely—if each time you go on the courts you spend a brief period analyzing your strokes, reviewing the basic fundamentals of form and working, if only for a few minutes, on areas where you have become sloppy. It is amazing how quickly we fall into sloppy habits, how easily we forget about follow-through or weight shift, how careless we become when we are more concerned about the point than the play. Points come with practice, and nowhere is this more true than in the case of the serve.

Since the first rule in tennis is get the ball into play, and the ball is first put in play via the serve, the importance of the stroke is obvious. In top tournament play, particularly among men, the emphasis on the serve is enormous. First-rank players consistently win their serves—an expression which means they win the game in which they serve. Losing the serve, which is also known as a service break, can be the deciding factor in a match. The reason is that the server has a definite advantage over the receiver: he initially puts the ball into play, and he puts it where he wants it to go. If he can consistently control its speed, spin and direction, he has a better than 75 percent chance of winning the point.

In club play, on the other hand, particularly at the intermediate level and below, it often appears to be a disadvantage rather than an advantage to serve. Losing the serve seems more common than winning it. Take a look at the players at your club, particularly during a ladies' day or round robin. Note how often the serve is lost instead of won. Spend a morning or an afternoon observing the variety of serves, and the contortions that precede them. You will probably see more different styles and eccentricities here than in any other stroke. Do this *before* you attempt your first serve. Observation is invaluable in clarifying in your own mind just what the serve is all about and what you should try and avoid.

Now, go back to the mirror even if the idea revolts you. It is a major aid in learning an effective serve. Stand far enough away from it to avoid seven years' bad luck, and from the furniture to avoid today's catastrophe. If you are particularly tall, or if your ceilings are particularly low, move the mirror outdoors. (I took out one overhead fixture and a sizable piece of plaster practicing this exercise indoors.) Again, assume that the mirror is the net. Stand sideways to it with your left foot about 3 inches behind an imaginary base line and at about a 45-degree angle to it. Place your right foot about 18 inches behind your left and parallel to the base line. Your body should not be square to the net when serving any more than it should be in the other strokes.

The serve is the nemesis of most beginners. This is the correct position.

Although most advanced players use a Continental or full Eastern backhand grip for the serve, you are not an advanced player and therefore are not capable of doing a good job with this grip. Use instead an Eastern forehand grip, your hand close to the butt of the handle. You might try extending your forefinger along the racket for added power. Raise your elbow so that it projects vertically into the air and let the racket hang loosely behind your back. Dangle it there, flexing your wrist as if you were trying to scratch your back with the racket head. This should be a loose motion. Check in the mirror that the racket is extended almost vertically behind your back, and that your elbow is straight up in the air rather than at right angles to your body. This sounds simple, and should be, but for many beginners, especially women, it is not. Unless they are athletically inclined or naturally loose-jointed, placing the arm behind the shoulder with the elbow extended vertically not only feels awkward but can actually be painful. This is purely a temporary condition and with a little practice can be quickly corrected. Your shoulder will loosen swiftly if you repeat this exercise ten or twelve times once or twice daily for a few days.

The serving motion involves rotating the arm in the socket so that the racket is literally thrown upwards and forward from this dangling position behind the back. In actual service, this "back-scratching" position, which is considered one of the most common points of good form in the serve, is achieved through a backswing. If you were simply to raise your elbow and drop the racket behind your back at the beginning of the serve, you would not only lose the sense of rhythm which is essential to smooth service, but you would also greatly re-

110

Eastern forehand grip is best for beginners.

Incorrect service position: the hippy serve. Note protruding right hip.

Bring racket back so that butt is vertical.

Racket should hang vertically behind back.

Another beginner's classic is The Yo-Yo.
Down and . . .

. . . up.

A common service error, sometimes called the shot-put serve, occurs when the elbow leads the racket, as demonstrated above, against fence. Correct serve has racket leading elbow to fence, below.

duce the thrust of your forward-throwing motion by being forced to begin it from a dead stop. The proper beginning for the backswing, therefore, is to aim the head of the racket, at about chest height, in the direction you eventually want the ball to go. In a sense, you are sighting the racket head in on the target.

Your stance should be fairly erect at this stage. It is not necessary to crouch forward, to stick out your right hip or rear end, or to lock your left knee as you are ready for the backswing. You should be comfortably relaxed and relatively upright with your weight evenly distributed on both feet. As you begin the backswing, bring the racket down along your right side so that the head passes at about knee height, and then moves up and out as if it were pointing at the corner of the rear and side fences behind you. As the racket head comes up, your elbow should move up and in towards your body and your wrist should flip back so that your racket drops down behind your back. As soon as it has dropped completely—without a pause or "hitch"—the upward and forward motion of the racket is begun. This should all be one smooth, uninterrupted sequence. The motion is exactly comparable to that of a pitcher throwing a ball.

As you bring the racket up and forward, your weight will naturally shift and your body will pivot so that it turns towards the net. At the same time your racket describes a full arc up, forward and down, and your follow-through ends alongside your left knee. (The exception is in the American Twist serve which you need not worry about for years and years.) This is all one fluid, uninterrupted motion. You will best understand it if you can actually watch it, which is

Poor: Note wrist position and racket angle.

Improved: Racket dropped, wrist coiled.

why the mirror is so valuable at this initial stage in learning the serve. If you jerk, or hesitate or stop the swing midway, the timing of the stroke will be broken. If you end with your racket still up in the air, pointed at the net or down alongside your right sneaker, go back and start again. Check your movements in the mirror until you find out what you are doing wrong.

As you bring the racket up and forward, you should have the feeling that if you let go, the racket would go sailing straight towards the mirror. If you do let go, it will, and you will have a mess, so hang on to your grip . . . at least until you get on the court. Once there, if you have an old racket, an excellent exercise for getting the feeling of the throwing motion in the serve is to throw the racket as hard as you can towards the opposite court. Stand behind the base line in the right court about a foot to the right of the center line. Make your backswing and foreswing as you did before the mirror, but just as the racket reaches its highest point and begins to move forward, release your grip on the handle. If your throwing motion has been smooth and uninterrupted, the racket should sail cross-court into the opposite service area. If it crashes instead at your feet

or flips inside your own service line, you have undoubtedly jerked your forward swing or released the racket too late. Your friends may think you crazy if they find you flinging rackets across the net, but ignore them. This is one of the best shortcuts to developing the feeling of the serve, as well as to conditioning your arm and shoulder to the motion.

Note the action of your wrist as you fling the racket upward. In all the other strokes you have learned to date, great emphasis has been placed on keeping the wrist firm. The serve is the big exception. When serving, your wrist must be flexible so that it actually snaps forward as the racket is thrown towards the net. You cannot achieve this snapping motion with a locked wrist.

Your feet are also involved in the serve, and they play a considerably more important role than many people believe. Most beginners and intermediates do terrible things with their feet, many of which are illegal. Foot-faulting is commonplace in weekend tennis. In most cases, it is unintentional, the result of carelessness and poor form. But it is illegal to step on any part of the base line, even with the tip of the toe, when serving. It is illegal to swing a foot across the base line, even if the foot does not actually touch ground, *before* the ball

An exaggerated way to learn coil and wrist snap is to hit ball with opposite side of racket.

Position on balls of feet gives power to serve.

is struck. (You can swing everything across afterwards, but it is usually not advisable.) It is also illegal to jump in the air so that both feet leave the ground during the serve, even if they remain behind the base line. Many top players appear to do this—specifically to raise their right foot in the air and bring it forward during the serve—but in most cases this actually happens *after* the ball has been struck and is a preliminary to rushing to net behind the serve. It is not a beginner's or intermediate's tactic and will only lead to foot-faulting and sloppy habits.

Again, use the mirror but this time watch what happens to your feet as you bring the racket up and forward. As your body rotates towards the net, your heels should rise up off the ground and you should pivot on the balls of both feet towards the net. At the completion of the follow-through, you should be fully

balanced and steady on your feet. If instead you find yourself falling into the court, try again. In your case, this is not a preliminary to rushing to net behind the serve, but rather an indication of improper stance. Experiment, watching your feet, as you strike an imaginary ball. Note that you achieve a greater reach as well as more power in your swing by getting up on your toes.

As impatient as you may be at this point to hit something more realistic than that imaginary ball, stick to this exercise without the ball for at least a few days, going through the full motion a dozen or so times in each session. There are several reasons for this. The first is therapeutic. You will feel stiff in the shoulder when you begin the exercise. By considering it as much a conditioning exercise to eliminate this stiffness as training to develop a fluid, smooth and uninterrupted stroke, you will be creating a foundation for the completed serve. Just as in the case of the ground strokes, you cannot build a good serve on a poor foundation. If you get the preliminaries down solidly, you can move to the next step with ease.

If you begin hitting a ball in the serve immediately, before your shoulder has become conditioned to the motion, the slight extra effort demanded by the ball may be just enough to discourage you into compromising your form. This happens especially with women, who give up on the shoulder rotation at the first twinge of pain and spend the rest of their lives potching ineffectual marshmallows from a stance square to the net. You may have some discomfort when you first begin the serving exercises. (When you ride a horse for the first time, you feel stiff too, but it goes away after a few sessions in the saddle.) You will have even more discomfort if you start out practicing the serve with a ball. But the discomfort will go away as soon as your shoulder loosens up, and it will loosen up with just a little preliminary practice.

Another reason to postpone introduction of the ball is to give you time to perfect a full, smooth swing without the distraction of also trying to hit the ball. Without the ball, you can concentrate on the swing, on the movement of your body, on the positioning of your feet, totally free of the pressure of also trying to send the ball across the net. You will also avoid a problem that has been fostered, albeit unintentionally, by many professionals. That is intellectualizing, or breaking down the simple throwing motion of the serve into so many specific elements that you become hopelessly confused. When teaching children, an instructor simply says:

"Watch how I do this and do it the same way." When teaching adults, he invariably attempts to explain each individual structural part of the stroke until the whole thing becomes so complex that even a computer would balk at digesting it.

This was a serious problem for me and it kept my serve in a state of virtual strangulation for most of that first summer. I had dissected its various parts so thoroughly that I was helpless to put them all back together again. The result was that instead of one smooth, throwing motion, I wound up with a series of individual motions that made any sense of timing or rhythm impossible. Because I started out with a ball right away, I was further impeded by the need to concentrate on hitting it.

The tournaments were almost upon me before I was finally extricated from what had seemed an insoluble problem. First the ball was eliminated. Then the racket-tossing exercise was introduced. Since I was an extreme case, we did not even start by throwing the racket across the net. More drastic effort was indicated. I was stationed near the base of a tall pine tree and told to throw the racket as high as I could into the topmost branches. (It is not advisable to use your brand-new $90 racket for this.) What this radical approach did for me was to force me to snap my wrist and loosen my arm and shoulder. The exercise succeeded in taking the various disjointed parts of my backswing and throwing motion and putting them back together again. I then proceeded to throw the racket over the net. Only when the stroke was absolutely smooth was I permitted to again use a ball.

One of the best arguments for delaying use of the ball is that for many beginners the toss is actually more difficult than the throwing motion with the racket. To try to learn both at the same time is like trying to rub your tummy and pat your head simultaneously. It is one more handicap you do not need. Only after you have completely mastered the backswing and forward swing of your racket so that you no longer have to think consciously of the motion should you consider using the ball.

The toss is the most critical part of the serve. Beginners would have much less trouble with their serves if they recognized this fact, but a surprising number ignore it. Again, the best place to observe this is at your own club. Concentrate on one person and note how often he tosses the ball in exactly the same spot. The chances are it is not often at all. Beginners and intermediates and even good players with a poor serve are inconsistent in their toss of the ball. They throw it up too soon or not soon enough, too high or to low, too far behind them or in front of them, too much to the left or to the right. If they followed any one of these patterns regularly, they could probably adapt their swing to it (although this is not desirable), but regularity is rarely a characteristic of the poor serve. Instead the ball is tossed to a different place every time so that there is absolutely no control of its direction when the racket finally hits it.

A cardinal rule of the toss, and one which is seldom stressed strongly enough, is: *Do not swing at your toss; toss to your swing.* In other words, do not toss the ball in the air and then swing at it. The proper sequence is to start your swing and then, as the racket is coming up, toss your ball to the spot where the racket will hit it easiest above your head. If you have already grooved a smooth, consistent swing, your racket will follow the same arc each time. Logically then, you will make your toss to the same point each time so that it coincides with the path of the racket. There is an analogy to this in skeet shooting. The clay target in skeet follows a predefined course. The shooter on station waits in a position so that his gun is ready to be aimed directly at a point along the path that the target will follow. He synchronizes the flight pattern of the target with a point of aim best suited to the angle of his position. His shot charge thus intercepts the clay bird on its predetermined flight path.

In tennis as in skeet, synchronization and timing are essential, and neither comes instinctively except to a gifted few. Since this book is not written for those fortunate souls but for people like you and me to whom nothing comes naturally, plan on considerable practice before you master the toss. It is tough. If you do not accept that from the start, it will lick you. It need not if you are willing to spend a little time developing it. To begin with, the toss should not be fancy. It is not necessary to wave the ball about or move your hand up and down as if it were a piston. Hold the ball with the thumb and fingertips of your left hand. Your palm should be upright and your fingers straight. If you clasp the ball with a witch's claw, you will never be able to release it. The ball should not be lower than your waist or higher than your chest at the beginning of the toss. Then lift the ball straight up as far as you can extend your arm and release it so that momentum carries it a few feet farther.

Do not loft the ball into the clouds.

Incorrect hand position for service toss. Note typical beginner's wrist flick.

Correcting a wrist flick in toss. By turning hand counterclockwise (back of hand facing server) wrist flick can be eliminated.

Correct hand position for service toss is achieved after practicing exercise in top picture.

It should be tossed to a point that coincides with the highest point your racket can comfortably reach, along the path that your racket will follow. For a reliable beginner/intermediate serve with the Eastern forehand grip, this will be in front of you, at a point just over the base line. At the end of the toss, the ball will pause for an instant before beginning its descent; ideally, this is when your racket should meet it. I said ideally. It takes considerable practice to make this ideal a reality. Obviously timing is a major factor. So is rhythm. But with practice, particularly if you have a solidly grooved service stroke, you *can* put the two together and come up with an acceptable, reliable serve. And you can do this the first season you play. The serve defeats the beginner more than any other stroke, but it is the one stroke that he can work on alone, without even a court. It pays the biggest dividends for practice of any stroke and is worth at least 50 percent of your learning efforts in the beginning stages of play.

Like every other stroke you have learned, the serve has a whole set of pitfalls. Perhaps the most common is unnecessary expenditure of effort. Go back to your club courts again and look at the exaggerated preliminaries and contortions many players go through before serving. There is the jumping jack who bobs up and down in a series of deep knee bends before beginning the backswing. There is the windmiller who winds up like a whirling dervish during the backswing and toss. There is the courtier who goes into a deep bow before starting the backswing. Notice how many people flail their arms about in purposeless motion and fancy flourishes. Aside from the fact that most of this motion serves no purpose, it is also exhausting. A good serve is characterized by economy of movement. It should look effortless and it should feel that way. It is not the brute strength with which the ball is hit but rather the *way* it is hit that puts it soundly into your opponent's service court.

The next most common pitfall in the serve is hitting a bad toss. If you have tossed the ball wide or short or too high or anywhere but where it should be tossed, let it fall and toss it again. This is perfectly legal and only sensible as far as you are concerned. If you hit a bad toss, you will make a bad serve. It will go either into the net or out of the service area and you have immediately reduced your scoring chances. Do not be embarrassed about repeating the toss two or three or more times. And do not let an impatient opponent psych you

into hitting a bad toss. Forget about his dirty looks and continue trying for a good one. Remember there is no reason ever to hit a bad toss.

Keep your eye on the ball. Although this point is stressed for every stroke, for some reason many people do not think it applies to the serve. If you want to hit anything, you must look at it—whether you are hitting a nail with a hammer, a rattlesnake with a rock or a golf ball with a club. This most certainly applies to the serve. Your eyes should not leave the ball from the first moment of the toss to the point at which it is struck. This is a particular pitfall of a toss that is too high. Aside from the fact that timing the swing to hit a falling ball is much more difficult than tossing the ball to the swing, when the ball is in the air so long there is a strong tendency to glance at your opponent's court to see where you are going to hit the ball. This is fatal. The only place your eyes should be is on the ball—as it leaves your racket, as it crosses into your opponent's court, as it leaves his racket and returns to yours. They should not be on him, on his court, on the net, on the ground or on your left sneaker. Not, that is, if you want to put the ball where it belongs.

Do not try to murder the ball. You will see amateurs at any club in the country smashing away at balls as if they were trying to rip the covers off them. Somehow they confuse this with the professional's big serve when it is really only a big laugh—for the opposition. It is much more important to develop a sound, reliable serve than a spectacular-looking one that consistently smashes into the net or over the fence. The latter may look good to you, to your mother, to your girlfriend and to a few other uninitiates, but it will look even better to your opponents since it is worth a point to them every time and a big zilch to you. Of course, even the most erratic server occasionally connects with a cannonball, but this is luck not skill. You have nothing to boast about if you miss-serve six for every one that makes it into the box.

Remember, getting the ball in play is the first rule of the game. Work on a serve that goes in every time, the *first* time. You will hear a great many players speak of first and second serves as if there was a mysterious difference between the two. The only mystery involved is why anyone would deliberately try to make his second serve even worse than his first serve. A double-fault is a point thrown away. It is the Inexcusable Inexcusable of tennis and there is almost never reason for it to occur.

More than one double-fault in a match should send you posthaste to the basket of balls and some workouts on the serve. It should also make you start asking some questions such as: What is wrong with both your serves, if you have two serves? And if you do, why do you? If you have typical club-type first and second serves, your first is probably an aborted cannonball and your second a bloopy marshmallow that even your six-year-old neighbor can handle with ease. Or it is so bloopy that he does not have to handle it at all because it has fallen on your side of the net. Then you have really blown it.

The answer is that for the first few years of play, and until you are ready to move on to another plateau in the serve, there should be no appreciable difference between your first and second serves. But there is vast difference, you say, having studied this carefully

during a televised tournament from the Houston Astrodome, between Arthur Ashe's first and second serves. You are right. But there is also vast differences between you and Arthur Ashe. If there is not, stop reading and donate this book immediately to a sick friend. Ashe and most of the top professionals have perfected the big serve to a point where it is not only a killer but also a reliable, consistent one. They can afford to gamble on it in match play because it is a point scorer a good percentage of the time. But they cannot afford to gamble on it twice in the same serve. If their big one does not go in, they then turn to their less spectacular, but even more reliable, second serve. Their second serve, I might add, is normally several times better than the first serve of anybody in club-level play.

So unless you have a big serve that is as reliable and consistent as that of the pros, forget about smashing in aces. They will only bring you grief. Concentrate on a smooth, sound, consistent serve of modest speed and good control. Work on making the ball go where you want it to go: to the backhand, to the forehand, down the line, deep. Your ability to control the ball is much more important than the speed you put on it. If you develop a really controlled, dependable serve, it will go in 85 percent of the time on the first try. This has both physical and psychological advantages. First, it conserves your energy and keeps you fresh longer in the game. Second, it boosts your morale and often does just the opposite to the opposition.

If your first serve *is* dependable, *is* controlled and goes in 85 percent of the time—as it should if it meets the first two qualifications—the law of averages heavily favors its going in the second time. Figure it out yourself. With an 85 percent accurate first serve, you will only have to second-serve 15 percent of the time. Since this serve too is 85 percent accurate, you have almost total protection against double-faulting. Even more important, you have not served a second serve that is a setup for a putaway, as most club-level second-serve marshmallows are. So forget about developing two serves. Put your efforts into acquiring one that is *always* good, regardless of the number it bears, and regardless of whether it looks spectacular.

Do go out with a basket of balls whenever you have an opportunity to and groove your serve. Take along a Hula-Hoop. Hula-Hoop? Relic of another era though they may be. Hula-Hoops are still available and are a great training aid in all strokes but particularly in perfecting a good serve. Placed flat on the ground in the opposite service court, they act as specific targets into which to try to place your served balls. In serving from the right court to a right-handed opponent, the best place to serve the ball is to the

backhand. Place the Hula-Hoop at the backhand corner of the service area, inside the service lines but as close to them as possible. Now practice serving all your balls into the Hula-Hoop.

Keep score on every ten serves and count only those that land inside the hoop. Do the same when serving into the other court. Place the hoop in the backhand corner. After you can serve consistently into the hoop, move it to the forehand corner. It is interesting how much more precise you can become in directing your serve by using such a simple device. If you cannot locate a Hula-Hoop, draw a circle with chalk if you have a hard-surface court, or with talcum powder on a clay or grass court. Any crutch such as this that can help you to zero in on a particular objective should not be overlooked. As important as actual play is to the development of your skills and game, it is only half the story. Exercises and practice drills are very substantially the other half. Put them to work for you and watch the dividends roll in.

XIII. The Overhead Smash and Return of Serve

To the serve, which so totally over-shadows it because it is vital to playing all games, the overhead smash is a rich and delicate cousin. Delicate? How can a stroke that when successful is almost always a dramatic, surface-searing winner be called delicate? The answer is simple: the overhead smash is tough. It is virtually identical to the serve in its execution except that the backswing is greatly abbreviated. The backscratch is retained, and is important, but usually there is no time for the full arc of the backswing. The ball is generally coming down instead of going up, since most balls returned with the overhead smash are lob balls, but with a volley from close behind the net the ball may well be rising. In either case, the ball is hit over the head, usually at the maximum reach of the racket, and it is a shot that is either a putaway or a disaster. To make it successfully requires extraordinary timing, judgment and skill. There is no margin for error.

The three moves in preparing for an overhead smash are getting your racket back behind your head quickly, bringing your right foot back or your left foot forward, and pointing your left hand at the ball. You must then go up to meet the ball from this position so that your racket swings up and forward (as in the serve) as your left arm comes down and your weight pivots forward. The stroke is so similar to the serve that the best practice for it is simply to continue working on your serve. The major variable besides the abbreviated backswing is that in the serve, you toss the ball to your swing, whereas in the overhead smash, you must get in position so that your swing meets the ball. But the ball you meet in the serve is, in a sense, a motionless ball since you hit it at the top of its rise in that ephemeral instant when it hangs suspended in the air. The target for the overhead smash is moving, up or down, but it is definitely moving. Obviously the timing, rhythm and synchronization are even more critical than in the serve.

Again you *must* keep your eyes on the ball while it is approaching, while you are hitting it and as it is on your racket. Do not look at where you want to place it or even follow it immediately off your racket. The danger in the latter is that you will take your eyes off the ball at the moment of impact. Hold them

b) As in the serve, the racket is brought up and forward. Note eyes are on the ball at all times.

The Overhead Smash: a) The beginning is similar to the beginning of the "back-scratch" in the serve. Note this player does not point left hand towards ball.

c) At the point of contact with the ball, the arm is fully extended and racket face is angled slightly downward.

there on the racket one second longer, and do not worry about where the ball goes. If you watch it, hit it clean on the center of your strings and send it deep into your opponent's court, the odds are that you will have scored a winner. Always aim deep. The most common error in the overhead smash is putting the ball into the net. The most common reason for this is taking the eyes off the ball at the moment of impact.

This brief description of the overhead smash should be enough to convince you that it is not a shot for the beginner or the intermediate. Sometimes you have no choice but to attempt it. If you must, try to remember the points outlined above. But if the situation is borderline and you have a reasonable chance to run back so that you can be in position to take the ball after it has bounced, by all means do so. Even the great Bill Tilden did whenever he could.

Back pedaling is a vital element of the overhead smash.

Eyes must never leave ball as backward motion continues.

Eyes continue to follow ball throughout the stroke.

If getting the ball back into play is the object of the serve, keeping the ball in play is the object of the return of serve. Although this sounds logical enough, it is surprising how many club-level players do nothing about developing a good return of serve. They may have their ground strokes completely under control, they may have a dependable, consistent serve, but they regularly flub the return of serve.

The theory behind the server's advantage is his ability to control the speed and placement of the service ball to make it more difficult for the receiver to return. In weekend tennis, the ball is often difficult to return—for these reasons in the case of a good server, and in the case of a poor server, because neither he nor you nor anybody else has a clue as to where the ball will eventually land. If your arsenal of strokes is sound, and if you apply a little extra concentration, there is no reason why you should have problems returning either good or bad serves.

The return of serve is basically a forehand or backhand drive. Because the ball must bounce within the service area, you have an advantage in not having to chase it all over the court. If it is a slow ball, it should be returned with a normal drive. If the ball is faster, it is still returned as a drive but with a somewhat shortened backswing, since its own force will be sufficient to take it back over the net. If it is a cannonball, use no backswing at all but simply meet the ball ahead of you and block it back, keeping your wrist stiff and your grip tight. Remind yourself to squeeze the handle just before the point of impact between racket and ball so the racket does not twist in your hands. Even a weak, small woman can return a cannonball if she

remembers to hold on to the racket, to get her weight forward so she meets the ball well in front of her, and then to follow through. An abbreviated backswing does not mean an abbreviated follow-through. The follow-through is essential to every return of serve. It is especially essential with a hard serve if you want your return to land in the court and not over the fence.

Where you stand to receive serve varies with your opponent's serve. If you are facing someone whose customary serve is a weak blooper that falls midway between the service line and the net, obviously it makes no sense to stand behind the base line. If he has a strong, deep serve, behind the base line is exactly where you want to be. (For a really hard serve you may want to stand several feet behind the base line but be on guard that an unexpected short serve does not then catch you a mile from where you can reach it.) On a deep, but average-speed serve, your best position is probably on the base line or just inside it.

In the forehand court, stand closer to the alley than to the center line so that you can reach a wide forehand serve. You will still be able to step across to reach a serve that skims the center line. The reverse applies when receiving in the backhand court. Although the serve you have learned carries no "first" or "second" labels (if it does, go back and review the chapter on the Serve), most of the opponents you will meet probably use two serves, so be prepared for the soft, bloopy second serve by standing in a little closer to the service line to receive it.

The ready position is extremely important in receiving serve. You should be on the balls of your feet, heels off the ground, and ready to spring either left or right as soon as you determine the direction of the ball. The racket should be held loosely in your hands so that it can be shifted quickly to the backhand grip if required. When you watch those professional matches on television, note how many of the top players jump with both feet off the ground just as the serve is made. This is a deliberate trick to keep them alert and start them moving towards the direction of the ball the instant it leaves the strings of the opponent's racket. It is a professional trick that works equally well for beginners. At no time when awaiting serve should your feet be planted flat on the ground. Most receivers also bend their knees and crouch slightly. The word is *slightly*.

Regardless of whether the serve is soft, medium or hard, the ball should be hit well out in front of you with your weight forward and your body sideways to the net. Your position for return of serve should be exactly the same as for a ground stroke. Many beginners and intermediates forget this and remain square to the net in returning serve. If this position does not work in a normal drive, there is no reason why it should work in the return of serve. And it does not. The slight jump at the time of serve is particularly helpful in launching your body into proper stroking position for the return.

Probably the most important factor in returning serve is watching the ball. If you are beginning to be bored by the constant repetition of this advice, I make no apologies. It is a message that cannot be repeated too frequently in tennis. It is one you should remind yourself of every time you assume the ready position to receive serve. Remind yourself especially if your opponent is one of the multimovement specialists who incorporates a distracting touch of choreography into every serve.

If you are watching your opponent's flailing arms or dipping knees or yo-yo exercises instead of specifically concentrating on the ball he or she is performing them with, you will seriously impede your reaction time in getting into position to return it. No matter what gyrations the server goes through, focus your eyes only on the ball. This is the number-one key to successfully returning serve because if you keep your eyes fixed on the ball, you will know where it is going the instant it leaves the strings of the racket and you will be able to move immediately in that direction. If, on the other hand, you permit anything to distract you from the ball until it is already part-way to the net, you will lose valuable positioning time and your advantage as receiver.

Once you have returned the serve, get back as quickly as possible into position for the next ball. In singles, if you have been pulled wide out of the forehand or backhand court, get back to the center of the court as fast as you can. In doubles, get back to wherever you should be in relation to your partner so the court has maximum coverage. Under no circumstances remain transfixed in the position from which you hit the ball, looking fondly or disbelievingly after it as so many beginners do. It may have been a beautiful return of serve but if it was not a winner—and few beginning and intermediate returns of serve are—you can be sure that it *will* be for your opponent. The most beautiful return of serve is worth exactly zero if it lands back in your court out of reach of your racket.

The best practice for developing a

good return of serve is to return as many serves as possible. The best way to do this is to work with a friend so that you can combine practicing return of serve along with the serve itself. While your partner serves a basket of balls from the opposite court, you can practice returning them. He should not try to hit your return but should concentrate only on serves until the basket is empty. After he has served a full basket from both the forehand and backhand courts, switch so that you serve and he returns. You can do more to refine both your serve and your return of serve in a half-hour of this kind of practice than in hours of game play.

Do not give up if you cannot enlist someone to practice with you. The next time you see anyone on the courts serving a basket of balls, even if it is the club champion, ask if he would object to your returning them to him. The chances are he will not, since this saves him a trip to the other side of the court to gather up the balls he has served there. And if he is very much above your level, or has an especially hard serve, this will give you excellent experience in learning how to handle hard serves.

Most beginners are psyched out by a very fast serve, principally because they lack the confidence to handle it. As a result, they mentally give up on it. One of the greatest fallacies in tennis, according to Bill Tilden, is the belief that a very fast serve is hard to return. It is actually easier to turn the speed of a fast serve back at the server than to

return a soft serve, *provided* you can reach the fast ball and get your racket face against it. If your eyes are fixed on the ball, not on the server, and you move the instant the ball leaves his racket, you should be able to get into position regardless of how fast the ball is traveling. Then you have only to put out your racket, grip it tightly and let the speed of the ball do the work. If your eyes have stayed with the ball and you have hung on to the racket and followed through, the ball should go back over the net as it is supposed to. But if you flinch, or look away at the moment of impact or back up because of the speed of the ball, score one for the other side.

If fast serves consistently undo you, try this exercise. You will need the help of someone who can serve a fast ball. Without your racket, get into the ready position to return it. As the ball is served, turn sideways, exactly as you would to return it with a racket, but try to catch the ball with your bare hand instead. You will be amazed at how fast a serve can be caught this way without hurting your hand. You will also note a couple of other things. Without a racket, you will instinctively move forward to catch the ball. You will not take a backswing with your arm because the natural catching motion is forward, not backward. Your eyes will also follow the ball into your hand because you cannot catch it if you look away. Try catching a few serves this way and then go back to returning them with the racket. The results should pleasantly surprise you.

XIV. Strategy

The balance, grips and strokes described in the previous chapters will provide you with three of the four basic elements of a sound tennis game. The fourth and final element is strategy. Regardless of whether you are playing your first game, your fiftieth or your five hundredth, there is only one strategy that makes any sense: *get the ball over the net.*

Even in top-level tennis, more than 70 percent of the points scored are the result of errors. Among beginners and intermediates, Welby Van Horn estimates that errors outnumber placements at least twenty to one. With that kind of odds, there is only one logical course: play with them. If you are serving, make sure the ball goes in not now and then but *every* time. If you are receiving or your serve is being returned, make sure you get the ball back over the net and into the opposite court.

The ideal is to do so with a well-executed cross-court drive, but you may not always be able to make one. Do not give up. Get your racket on the ball any way you can. Lunge for it. Reach for it. Scramble for it. It is remarkable how many balls you can reach if you make

up your mind that you are going to get to every one. Regardless of how impossibly out of range a ball may seem, stick out your racket and try. You may not make a beautiful shot or look very good in the process, but if your ball goes over, even as a bloop, you have given the other fellow another chance to blow the shot.

If you can get into position to return the ball with a proper stroke, by all means make every effort to do so. It is bound to be a better shot than the one you barely managed to scoop over the net. Concentrate on returning every ball so that it clears the net by about 3 feet and lands deep in the opposite court. Forget about speed and fancy placements. Steadiness is considerably more important in beginning tennis.

A player who manages to get the ball back time after time has the law of averages on his side. It is surprising how many new players forget or ignore this dictum. They often react in either of two ways: they become impatient to end the point and so attempt to put the ball away—almost always a disaster; or they just give up on it entirely. Defeatism is more likely in the case of a very short

A good backhand drive position, showing how anticipation, concentration and footwork bring results.

or a very long ball. The novice player often does not make the little bit of extra effort required to run to the ball and get his racket on it, but simply quits. If he stretched himself, he would get the ball back at least sometimes. But if he stands and watches it bounce, he will never get it back.

Aside from the strokes themselves, there are three distinct elements involved in getting the ball back: antici-pation, concentration and footwork. Although that is probably the best order in which to put them, the three cannot really be separated since they are totally interdependent. Anticipation is the most elusive, and so the most diffi-cult. It is the ability to determine where the ball is going before it gets there so that you can move to it and get into position to hit it without scrambling.

The next time you watch tournament

tennis, note how unhurried the players seem to be. They move easily and unrushed towards the ball, with time to get into position and to make careful deliberate strokes. In contrast, weekend players always seems to be dashing madly after balls that are just out of reach. The reason for the difference is primarily anticipation.

Most novice players wait until the ball has crossed the net and bounced in their court before they begin to move to it. As they progress, they may begin to move as the ball is crossing the net. But even this is not soon enough. A top player, on the other hand, reacts the instant the ball leaves the strings of his opponent's racket. He determines where the ball is going and begins moving immediately. The route he takes to the ball is the shortest one—the obvious road but one rarely traveled by the novice. The weekend player more often moves to the side and then forward, or forward and then to the side, rather than along a diagonal (and therefore shorter) plane directly to the ball. Instant recognition of where the ball is going to bounce and the fastest way to reach it comes with experience, which is why a beginner's anticipation is generally so poor. It is less a question of reflexes, as many older beginners believe, than of concentration.

You cannot see the ball come off your opponent's strings unless your entire attention is focused on it. You may think you are concentrating on the ball but in reality a hundred other elements may be diverting your attention from it. The most common is your opponent. But court noises, other players, spectators, wind blowing through nearby trees, a butterfly, thoughts of last night's dinner or today's grocery list or a prospective account at the office, a sneaker that is pinching and myriad other physical or mental distractions also interfere with your ability to concentrate on the ball. Concentration is not a static element. It fluctuates as the distractions fluctuate. And for some mysterious reason, novice players are far more subject to distraction than advanced ones. Perhaps it is more accurate to say that players advance in ability as their ability to concentrate improves.

Imagine the distractions of center court at Forest Hills. The stands and boxes are packed with spectators who come and go and applaud and often cheer. The giant electrically lighted marquee records every point and is a constant reminder of the game and set scores. The press boxes are filled with clacking typewriters, teletypes and telephones. A television crew records each stroke, and behind glass windows at the rear of one end of the court, waiters serve lunch to members of the U.S. Open Club. There are umpires on every line and straight-backed ball boys and ball girls standing alongside the net to chase down balls. Coaches, photographers, reporters, United States Lawn Tennis Association officials stand in little crowds on the grass. Yet those who play on the center court at Forest Hills see only the ball. Their ability to concentrate totally on the game, to block out all other distractions and extraneous elements, to detach themselves entirely from everything but the play at hand, is one reason why they got there in the first place. Tennis demands total concentration. Champions achieve it; novices rarely do.

There is no magic in being able to concentrate. It is something any player can learn if he is really determined. Youngsters have an advantage here because their minds are less cluttered than adults' and they are therefore prone to fewer mental distractions. But there is no reason why older people, once they understand the importance and necessity of concentration, cannot attain the same mental focus on the ball. There are some tricks that help. Playing late in the evening, in poor light, helped me considerably when I first tackled the sport. In order to see the ball at all, I had to rivet my attention to it. If I glanced away for one second, the ball was lost and I had no hope of picking it up in the dim light. I am reminded of this each time we hold a Friday evening Round Robin at Gipsy Trail. Our courts are still unlighted and the play generally goes on until the last faint shimmer of light is gone. It becomes increasingly difficult to see the ball and increasingly more important to focus every shred of one's attention on it. I am always surprised and pleased at how effective an exercise in concentration this is, and how markedly my game picks up as a result of it.

Keeping your eye on the ball when it leaves your opponent's racket is only part of concentration. You must also keep your eye on the ball throughout its entire flight, including the moments when it makes contact with, remains in contact with and leaves the strings of your racket. How many times have you been told this now? Not often enough, I suspect. If you are a typical weekend player, there are probably more times than you can count when you have watched the ball come off your opponent's racket, followed it through its bounce and beyond, gotten into position for a perfect stroke—and *flubbed* the ball into the net, out of the court or straight up into the air with a painful

ping of wood or metal. You committed the cardinal sin of tennis. You looked away just at the moment you hit the ball. You took your eyes off the ball for one fleeting instant to see where it was going to go, or what your opponent was doing or for some other reason you can't define or identify. It only takes one fleeting instant to goof the shot. It happens every day at every level of play but it happens most often to the novice because his powers of concentration are not developed. He can be reminded a thousand times; he can tell himself over and over again *eyes on the ball,* but still he will look away just at the critical moment. And he almost never knows that he has done so.

Again, there are some tricks that help. I painted a circle 4 inches in diameter on the center of the strings of my racket to force myself to watch the ball and

Painting a sweet spot on strings is an aid to concentration.

racket connect. It also helped me to meet the ball with the center of the strings rather than off center. This trick was so successful that I have painted circles, in either red or blue ink, on the strings of my children's rackets. Their games have improved measurably as a result. For desperate cases, there is another trick that is effective. Have an old racket frame only partly strung so that there are six lengthwise and six cross strings. This leaves a hittable area closely approximating the sweet spot in the center of the racket with four air spaces around it. With such a weird arrangement, either you hit the ball exactly on the center of the racket, or it passes through the holes in the strings or plops to the ground. If you hit squarely on the center of the strings, however, the ball bounds off as it would on a normally strung racket. The trick here is that you cannot hit squarely unless your eyes are on the ball.

Another trick which many players use to advantage is concentrating on actually seeing the seams on the ball. If this sounds farfetched, try it. You will be surprised that you can see them if you really concentrate—but you must really concentrate in order to see them. Some manufacturers make balls with seams of a different color. If you can find these, try them. They can be a useful aid in helping to develop concentration.

The number-one aid to concentration, however, is to leave everything else on the sidelines when you walk on the court. This applies to your home, office, social and personal concerns. Tennis is a game that makes mental as well as physical demands. To enjoy it to the fullest, you must put as much of yourself, mentally as well as physically, into it as you can. When you are on the court, for-

get everything except getting to the ball and sending it back.

The way you move on the court has a lot to do with how fast you reach the ball and how easily you get into position to send it back. If you have been told a thousand times to keep your eye on the ball, you have probably been told five hundred times to keep your feet moving. The only person I have ever seen in my realm of play who is an exception to this rule is Erza Hartman, who can play an entire game without, it seems, moving out of a circle about 6 feet in diameter. But Erza is, as stated earlier in these chapters, both a remarkable tennis player and an extraordinary person. Her game is one of wits and perfect placements, a combination which inevitably traps her opponent into rushing from one side of the court to the other while returning every ball to her feet. Since a half-volley made with a Western grip is Erza's favorite shot, she sends it back again, always to a place where her opponent is not. I have seen her defeat hot-shot college players fifty years her junior with her remarkable control of the ball. More accurately, I have seen them exhaust themselves in sweaty disbelief at their inability to cope with this tiny elderly lady.

But the very uniqueness of Erza and her game is why she is an exception to the rule. Over the years at Gipsy Trail, there has been no counterpart either to her or to her unorthodox strokes, which is why your chances of successfully playing Erza's stationary game are about as good as mine are for making center court at Forest Hills. As for her half-volley—forget it. Most people do not believe it when they see it. It works for her, but why is as mystifying as her game and her boundless energy. For the rest of us, to attempt to play rooted to one part of the court is to remain forever mired in defeat.

You must move, and the faster, the lighter, the more easily you do, the better will be your game. A player who can reach *every* ball has a chance to send every ball back. Assuming you have watched the ball and anticipated where it is going, the best way to get there is by short, bouncy steps. The ability to hop, skip and bounce on the court is the secret of reaching the ball in time to get into position to hit as orthodox and well-balanced a stroke as possible. Good players are never flat-footed. Their heels are never on the ground. Their weight is always on the balls of their feet. Watch them at a tournament or on television. They are in motion *all the time*, so that they can spring, jump, twist and adjust to any unexpected bounce of the ball. They are ready to move in any direction, to change direction, to reverse direction, upon an instant's notice.

Now watch the footwork of a novice player. If he is typical, he races to where he thinks the ball will be, then plants his feet in position and commits himself to that spot. If the ball bounces exactly where he expected it to, fine. But if his judgment is in error, or if the ball takes a funny bounce either because it carried spin or hit a bad spot on the court (ours are full of them), he is unable to alter position. He must then hit the ball too close, or reach to hit it too far away, or stoop or bend from the waist or go through some other contortion that will throw off his stroke and probably his shot.

If, on the other hand, he had been bouncing in small, springy hops, he could easily have moved back for the close ball or ahead for the long one, and still have made the best possible stroke from the best possible position. Good, bouncy footwork makes it possible to adjust to change of pace, crazy spins, drop-shots, long balls, wide balls, erratic balls and any idiosyncrasies of the court surface. It also keeps you alert so that you are moving towards the shot the moment the ball leaves your opponent's racket.

Your eyes should send constant messages to your feet. Your feet should respond with constant movement. As soon as you see a short ball that is going to drop just over the net, your feet must start forward. If you wait until the ball crosses the net, it will be too late to reach it. If you see that the ball is going wide, begin sidestepping towards it, directly to the right or left if it is a long ball, on a diagonal if it is shorter. The side step should be more a hop and a skip than a run. This assures that you will not be caught on the wrong foot when you reach the ball.

Never try to run backwards for a long ball because it will reduce your speed and throw you off balance. If you are caught at net at mid-court and the ball is headed for the base line, turn around and run for the base line until you are well behind the point at which the ball will bounce. You will be amazed at how many balls you can catch up to this way and still have time to get into position to return effectively. Unless you are certain that the ball is going out, assume that it is in and run for it. A lot of balls that bounce on the back tape could be returned for a point if just a little extra effort were made to reach them.

Also remember, never stretch for a wide ball if you can move into a better position to hit it properly. No matter

Moving back to take a long ball in good position.

Improvising to take a long ball: Running with back to net when necessary.

Pivoting into a forehand drive in good position.

Improvising: Stepping back on a close ball for better forehand drive position.

133

Improvising: Reaching for high (and prob-ably hopeless) return.

Improvising the volley return: Ball has been punched while square to net.

Improvising: This high ball was hit forehand at chest height.

Bending for the shot in a good forehand drive position.

how hard you try to be in perfect position for every shot, there are bound to be times when you have no choice but to improvise. The best players in the world do so, often. But when they do, it is generally because they have no other alternative. This is not always the case with the novice who, with a little more attention to footwork, could have avoided the unnecessary improvisation.

Do not cramp a stroke you could make smoothly by stepping away from the ball. Do not hit off the wrong foot and out of balance when you can hop onto the correct foot with proper weight balance by taking another step. Keep your knees flexed, your heels high and the balls of your feet bouncing at all times, even when you are tired. The best way to fight fatigue is to move. Once you plant your feet, you will begin to drag, which only increases your tiredness. The only time your feet should stop their constant bouncy motion is when you actually hit the ball. Then, since they have carried you into the most perfectly balanced position for the stroke, your ball should go over the net exactly where you want it to.

Some final thoughts about strategy. As your game improves and your control of the ball permits you to place it more precisely, do not fall into the trap of overconfidence. If you can consistently put the ball deep into your opponent's backhand corner, by all means do so. But if it goes out four times for every one time it goes in, you are making a strategic error every time you make this shot. You would be much wiser to send the ball safely down the middle and wait for your opponent to make the error. Or if your lob invariably goes out or lands just over the net for a setup, leave it out of your game until you have brought it under control in practice.

Concentrate on a simple, deep ball that always goes over, rather than on a tricky, fast one that only makes it sometimes. Welby Van Horn often said that the worst thing that can happen to a beginner is to make a great shot by mistake. Having done so, he then assumes that he has mastered the game and consequently tries to play over his head. Every new player makes an occasional great shot. He is not a great player until such shots can be made every time he attempts them. The steady, unflamboyant retriever who gets to every ball and sends it back is the one most likely to score points and win games. This is the single most important strategy any newcomer to the game can learn. Beginning tennis players start losing when they go on the offensive and start improvising. Resist the urge for glory in your first few seasons and settle instead for a defensive game that is based on a solid foundation and sound strokes. Practice what you have learned here, apply it on the courts, and remember, more trophies are won by this kind of game than by any other.

PART III: Etiquette and Rules

XV. Courtsmanship

A lot has been said in the previous pages about balance, grips, strokes and strategy. These four fundamentals form the foundation of tennis. With this foundation, regardless of your age and athletic ability, you can play tennis. You may not win games at first as Welby warned me when I returned from Puerto Rico, but you will have the tools with which to build a solid, dependable game. The pleasures they bring you will depend not only on how you develop and use them but also on how you disport yourself upon the courts. Tennis should be fun regardless of the level at which you play. If it is not, or if your reasons for playing are the wrong ones, you are doing an injustice to yourself and to the sport.

Most of the 20 million Americans playing tennis today are out on the courts because they enjoy the game, the people they play with, and the sense of physical exhilaration it brings them. It is a sport eminently suited to all ages and physical conditions that demands wits, skill and, to be fully appreciated, humor. Without the last, tennis becomes not so much a sport as a contest and some of its pleasures are reduced both for the player and for those he plays with. If

your only reason for playing is to prove prowess over your fellows, you will probably miss much of the fun of the game.

Tennis was never intended as a medium for venting one's anger or aggressions, although it can certainly provide a safety valve for clearing the heart and head in times of stress. Tennis will not take off weight (the pounds you lose in a game are usually water and invariably return with the next drink) but it will firm muscles and tighten flab. Tennis will not save an ailing marriage by forcing togetherness on the courts (if he did not want to play with you before, now that you have learned the game he is not likely to change his mind) but it is a wonderful way to meet new people and new partners. Tennis is a social as well as a sociable sport, one that you can play anywhere and enjoy indefinitely. You will enjoy it even more if you are familiar with some of the unwritten rules of the game.

Probably the single most important rule is to behave like a gentleman or lady. General Robert E. Lee defined a gentleman as "a man who never makes anyone feel inferior." He might have added: "and who is always well mannered." It is surprising how many people who *are* gentlemen and ladies off the courts cease to be during a tennis game. In many cases, I prefer to believe their behavior is the result of ignorance rather than intent. But some rules are so well defined that there is no excuse for not knowing them.

If your club or the courts on which you play have clothing rules, respect them. It is *gauche*—not *chic*—to show up in tennis yellows or tennis blues, even though they are popularly in vogue and acceptable elsewhere, if there is a "whites only" rule where you play. Whites only means white shirt, shorts, skirt, socks and tennis shoes. To wear any other color is exactly comparable to arriving at a formal dance in a sports jacket, or at church in a bathing suit.

Keep your outfits simple. There is nothing more distracting or annoying than to play with or against someone who is constantly adjusting a waistband, tucking in a shirt or pulling down an errant undergarment. To play with no shirt at all, or to strip off your shirt halfway through the game (unless you are Raquel) is bad form. (If you are Raquel, it is good form but still not done.) To play without socks if you are a man, or in deep décolletage if you are a woman, is also bad form. The femme fatale who bares herself to the navel every time she bends over to pick up a ball may attract attention but not respect. The same applies to skimpy underpants. At a Ladies' Day at Gipsy Trail, I was about to serve when my partner at net bent forward in an exaggerated ready position. To my dismay, she had *forgotten* her underpants! By all means, not only wear the proper attire but wear all of it.

If you must wear bandages, keep them to a minimum. The fellow who appears on the court wrapped like a newly exhumed Egyptian mummy is almost as disconcerting as the woman who forgets her underwear. It is often necessary for a player to wear an Ace bandage or elastic sleeve because of a sore elbow or weak knee, but rare is the player who is so disabled in every joint and limb that he must swath himself in yards and yards of surgical wrapping. If his physical condition is that bad, he belongs in the hospital, not on the tennis courts.

The only thing more annoying than an overbandaged opponent is one who chronicles each and every ache throughout the play. As he serves, he winces and cries out in pain. As he runs for a ball, he grimaces and groans. As he waits for your serve, he massages a shoulder, his face a contortion of agony. When asked if he would care to stop play, he usually replies negatively in the stoic tones of a martyr. If his suffering tends to soften your game, you have been had. Ignore the bandages if you can, and give him everything you have.

Be on time for tennis dates and especially for any matches you may play. Do not enter a tournament unless you are sure you will be able to play all the matches involved within the time span allotted to them. Because weather conditions in outdoor tournaments are never 100 percent predictable, try to play your matches as early in the allotted time span as possible so that you have alternate dates available if rained out. Be reasonable in setting up match dates. If you can shift a hair appointment or skip a luncheon in order to accommodate your opponent, do so. With a smile.

If you need warming-up time before a match (and most players at all levels do), schedule it with someone other than your opponent *before* the actual match time so that you are ready to meet your opponent on the court promptly at match time. It is customary at the beginning of a match to rally briefly with your opponent and also to take a few practice serves. Do not confuse this with warming up, or expect your opponent to perform the service for you. Enlist someone else for this job. If you need an hour to warm up, be at the courts a full hour before the scheduled tournament. If you need ten minutes, get there ten minutes before. Do not arrive just in time for the match and then expect your opponent to wait while you warm up.

Under no circumstances arrive *after* the scheduled match time, or delay its start so that your opponent is forced to wait once he has warmed up. Nothing can throw off one's game as badly as being forced to stand around getting cold and stiff after a vigorous warmup. Technically a player who does not show up within ten minutes of a scheduled tournament is considered to have defaulted, but in most clubs, exceptions are sometimes made to the rule, especially where extenuating circumstances exist. Certainly, however, you should advise your opponent as early as possible that you will be delayed. If you are going to be more than a few minutes late, you should by all means offer to default and leave the decision to your opponent. Although most people, particularly in social play, are sympathetic to a reasonable cause for delay when properly explained, there are really few circumstances which justify being late for a match.

An example of an unjustified circumstance occurred in one of our recent tournaments. A Ladies' Singles match was scheduled for 9:30 A.M., between a relatively new member and an aging self-styled swinger. The younger woman arrived at the courts at 8:45, checked out her equipment, balls, shoelaces and other accoutrements, then went on the court at 9 with a partner who agreed to warm her up for the half-hour she required. They hit ground strokes and volleys for twenty minutes and then practiced serves and return of serves for another ten. At 9:30 she was ready to begin play, an audience had gathered and an empty court stood waiting. At 9:40 the scene was the same. At 9:50 it was still the same. At 9:55, in exasperation, the young woman telephoned her opponent. Swinger was still in bed. To compound the inexcusable, instead of defaulting the match as she should have, she insisted upon throwing herself together and playing. By the time she arrived at the courts in a flurry of cutesy apologies, the younger woman was physically and psychologically devastated. Swinger won the match but lost the last slim shreds of respect she had at the club.

It is just as important to be on time for regular play as for match play, and just as discourteous to your partners to treat tennis dates in a cavalier manner. If you make a date for 9 A.M., be there at 9 A.M. If you cannot be, give your partner enough advance notice so he can make other plans. Arrive at the court with tennis balls, preferably ones that have not been in circulation since the Depression, teethed on by the dog or run over by the lawn mower. *Always* bring balls. You would not expect to drive a car without gas or shoot a gun without shells. There is no reason why you should expect to play tennis without balls, or assume that your partner is bringing them. Each of you should arrive with a can of balls that are matched and in reasonably good condition for play.

Which can is used depends upon a variety of circumstances. Yours probably will not be if it yields a tattle-tale gray Wilson, a clay-colored Dunlop and a yellow Spalding. Mixed breeds are invariably frowned upon. Matched sets that are so dirty they cannot be seen (you can wash them bright again in your washing machine but once or twice is maximum) and dead ones that do not bounce at all are equally unpopular. If you show up with any of these regularly, you will be too.

Another ploy that saves balls but loses friends is to stall opening a new can until your partner opens his. You then smile and say: "Since yours are open, we might as well use them." I know one woman at Gipsy Trail who carried the same unopened can for three seasons. She might be carrying it still except that the label said: "Choice of the 1968 USLTA National Open Championship." By 1972 people began to drop hints about the can being out of print.

If you do play with the other person's balls, have the courtesy at the end of the game to see that all three are collected from the court and returned to their owner. My two pet peeves about Ladies' Days at Gipsy Trail are that I always seem to be the only member of whatever four-woman team I am assigned to who brings balls, and that I always seem to go home with one or more of them missing. Everybody is happy to play with them, but rarely does anyone make an effort to help find them and return them to me after the game. The moment the play is ended, the other three walk off the court and I am left to do the scouting. One Ladies' Day I tried unsuccessfully to

change this pattern. I arrived, like the others, without balls. We wound up playing with three unmatched dogs discarded by the pro. I resigned myself to bringing my own balls.

At some clubs, new balls are provided to all the players at round-robins and on ladies' days. They are always provided at officially sanctioned tournaments, and are changed for fresh ones after a specific number of games. They may or may not be provided at club and public tournaments. When players have to provide their own balls for a match, each player should arrive with an *unopened* can of a standard brand. It is then customary for one set of balls to be used in the match. At the end of the play they are kept by the loser and the winner takes home the other, unopened balls, regardless of who brought which set originally.

Do not be a court hog. With tennis enjoying the biggest boom in its history, facilities in most parts of the country are lagging well behind demand. Everybody wants to play, especially on weekends. To assure that most people have a chance to, the majority of public and private courts have standardized rules that are posted for all to see. Some courts limit play to one hour for singles, one and a half hours for doubles. Others restrict play to two sets of singles, three of doubles. Some courts operate on a first-come, first-sign-up basis; others on drawings set at specific times. Some courts do not permit any signing up prior to the actual day of play; others permit long-range reservations. The system used is generally based upon the degree of demand, and every system leaves someone disgruntled.

When tennis was still an inner-circle sport at Gipsy Trail, the court aristocracy was so formidable that no lesser creature dared venture forth on a summer Saturday or Sunday between 9 and 11 A.M. and 3 and 6 P.M. The rationale was that if sunstroke time was not good enough for the duffers, they did not deserve to play at all. But times and tennis have changed at Gipsy Trail. Today the courts are filled on summer weekends from 8 in the morning to dark, and for every old face, there are dozens of new ones. The scramble at sign-up time each morning looks more like a one-cent sale at Filene's basement.

People arrive unshaven, uncombed, unfed, through mists still rising from the greenery surrounding the dew-covered courts. Many are still hung over from the previous night's festivities as they record their names, bleary-eyed, on sign-up cards. Promptly at 8 A.M. the club pro drops all the cards in a hat, shuffles them and draws them one by one. The first name to be drawn has first choice of court and time; the second, second choice, and so on. The names are then recorded in the proper slots on a chalk board that by mid-morning requires a computer to decipher.

For those too weak or too weary to make the morning melee, all hope is not lost. Occasionally, but only occasionally, someone fails to show up to claim his court. He is permitted a ten-minute grace period and then relinquishes his right to it. If one is prepared to sit diligently by the courts for most of the day, he has an outside chance of claiming such a court provided he is fast enough on his feet to beat the other seventeen players who will all sprint for it simultaneously at exactly nine minutes and fifty-nine seconds after the appointed hour. Since there are only two access gates to the courts, clever maneuvering during the critical first five minutes that a court is vacant is necessary to be in the best possible sprinting position to stake first claim.

Elaborate though such a system seems, it was necessitated, first, by the unprecedented demand for the courts this past season, and second, by some decided court hogs who managed to skillfully convert a more simplified system to shambles. Court Hog Number 1, who evidently slept on the clay in order to be first at sign-up, promptly tied up four of the five courts for the rest of the morning by signing his name and the names of all his relatives and friends. By cleverly switching and juggling partners at the end of each time allotment, they managed to keep a "new" team of doubles going on all four courts all morning long. They also managed to bring the tempers of those waiting on the sidelines to the level of eruption. Some simply stalked off in anger. Others ranted and raved until the beleaguered tennis pro decided on the new system. The Hog Pack still monopolizes most of the courts most of the mornings, but at least now, they all have to get up before breakfast to do so.

There are other ways to discourage court hogs but they are not entirely sporting. The question you must ask yourself is: Does one unsporting act deserve another? If your answer is yes, here are a few suggestions. If you have several small children, particularly ones who cry a lot, you can bring them to the courts for the morning. If you are feeling particularly mean, equip them with leftover New Year's Eve noisemakers. If they are older, station them on the opposite side of the court and have them inquire about dinner, when they can drive the car or any other subject that demands discussion. Give them detailed, specific answers. Repeat if they have trouble hearing you.

If you have a retriever, this is a perfect time to get in a little preseason training. Stand at one end of the fence and throw your training dummy as far as you can towards the other end. Send your dog to fetch, and then reward him profusely, and loudly, when he returns it to you. Do not hesitate to use your training whistle if the dog is accustomed to it. If your dog is not a retriever, he may still enjoy chasing tennis balls. If your friends have dogs too, invite them along. Bring one large bone and toss it up against the fence. If the fence is still standing after they all hit it en masse, it will undoubtedly be vibrating like a Greek zither.

Take this book and a movie camera to the court. Bring along a friend, preferably with a gravel voice. Station yourselves close to the fence. Point your camera at the players in action (film is not necessary for this ploy) while your friend audibly compares their balance, grips and strokes to those outlined in the book. Point out any deviations in form or execution. Expressions such as "Look at that collapsed wrist," "Make sure you get that over-the-shoulder follow-through," "Can you believe that backhand?" and "So that is what is meant by potching a serve" should send the deviation quota sky high. Do not hesitate to explain or analyze a player's form yourself. After all, you have read the book. And by all means, wince, grimace, shake your head, visibly shudder and say "Oh no" whenever someone misses a point. If the villains are still on the court by the time you weary of this act, leave slowly with an expression partway between illness and pain.

A less obvious ploy is simply to ask each court how long they have been playing. Do not expect honest answers. You may not get an answer at all. Be patient and ask the question again in about five minutes, preferably just as someone is about to serve. This can be varied by asking the set and game scores. You still may not get an answer. You may even get a tennis racket flung in your direction. If you are sensitive, take turns with your partner in asking the score. If you are really sensitive, forget about playing tennis and try some less popular sport.

And if you suspect you may be a court hog yourself, test the air a bit the next time you play. Are the players waiting the same ones who always seem to be waiting? Have they been a little cool to you lately? Do you always play in prime time when you could just as conveniently play at some other time, at least on occasion? If you can play during the week or evenings, do you still insist on regularly tying up a lot of weekend time? Remember that there is no better place to apply the Golden Rule than on the tennis courts.

When play is in progress, even though it may be Class D in quality, it is impolite to walk behind that court to get to or from your own. Wait outside the court until the point has been completed and then ask to be excused before passing. I have seen players who would not dream of trespassing on a court during a tournament or top level play, stride across one in the middle of a novice's serve. The rules of courtesy are the same at all levels of play. If there is any variation, it is that the better player should bow a little deeper to the beginner in order to encourage him.

When a ball from another court rolls

onto your court, stop play immediately and return it to its source. It is not good sportsmanship to continue the play regardless of who makes the point. It is definitely not good sportsmanship to claim interference after you have lost the point. If your ball rolls into another court, the proper way to ask for it back is to say: "Thank you, please." Many players are confused about when to say this. If the ball rolls behind the base line and does not interfere with the point in play, wait until the point is completed before calling "Thank you." If the ball interrupts play, as soon as the point is stopped, call "Thank you." If, on the other hand, the ball rolls unnoticed by the other players on their court and comes to rest directly behind the feet of one of the players, thereby constituting a safety hazard, it is correct to call "Thank you" and in so doing interrupt their point. Your interruption will be more appreciated than a sprained ankle.

Two other points of play create an unnecessary amount of confusion among intermediates as well as novices, principally because they are not sure of their specific responsibilities. The server is responsible for calling the score in games before he begins the game, and in points before he begins every point. This is his job at all times except when there is an umpire to call games and scores in his place. Since umpires are mainly used only in tournaments, the habit of always calling the score before your serve is one you should acquire early. Novices seem to have extraordinary difficulty keeping track of their scores. Women are true champions in this department. Much of the difficulty could be avoided if each server remembered to call out the score loudly and clearly before every toss of

the ball. Any discrepancies can then be noted immediately, and a lot of mental sulking about whether the score was right or wrong can be eliminated. This would also eliminate the particular annoyance, sometimes perpetrated innocently, sometimes deliberately, of having your opponent shout across the net for the score at exactly the moment you start to serve. It is your own fault if the ball goes in the net because he or she would not have had to ask if you had announced the score when you were supposed to.

Responsibility for calling balls out also causes both confusion and hard feelings more often than it should. Assuming again that there are no umpires or linesmen involved, the responsibility in singles for calling the serve in or out is solely the receiver's. He should make the call promptly and clearly and he should let the ball continue on out without swinging at it. The correct call is "fault" but in weekend play, "long" and "wide" are also commonly used. While not technically correct, they are often easier to announce quickly. It is unfair to your opponent to delay the call, to hit the ball back and then call it out, or to treat an ace as if it were out. The first two affect his timing. The second, his temper.

It is not necessary to call a ball that does not come over the net since your opponent will be all too well aware of the fact. It is necessary to call a "let," which is a ball that nicks the tape, sometimes so imperceptibly that it is audible only as a minor *ping*. If the ball then lands in the proper service court, it should be returned to the server with the remark "Take two," if it was a first serve; "Take one," if it was a second serve. A let ball that does not land in the proper service court counts as a fault and the call is "Take one" if a first serve; "Let, fault," if a second serve.

If a serve is so close that you cannot tell whether it is in or out, you have two alternatives: play it as if it were in, with a positive manner and no commentary; or let it go by and ask that your opponent please take the serve over. You should not poke the serve back half-heartedly, debating aloud whether it was in or not. Nor should you shift your responsibility to your opponent by asking his opinion. He is not in a position to make the judgment and should not be embarrassed into doing so. Nor should you ask your wife in the stands, the groundskeeper clipping hedges beyond the fence or the kid on the next court. It is your responsibility, and solely yours, to call the serve as accurately, as quickly and as confidently as you can and then to play or not play as the call dictates without further comment or distraction to your opponent.

The exception to this is in doubles when you are receiving. Then the responsibility for the call is your partner's. All you have to worry about is getting the ball back. It is his job to decide whether or not the serve is good. Just as in singles, if it is not, his call should be instant and authoritative, so that you do not unnecessarily disrupt the server's timing by returning out balls. If the call is slow, or late or hesitant, you have no choice but to hit the ball. Treat every ball you receive in doubles as a good ball unless you are told otherwise. If you hesitate, waiting for your partner's call, it will throw off your timing and consequently your return. Obviously the same rules apply when your partner is receiving and you are making the calls.

Make your call promptly and confi-

dently. Just as it is poor form to ask another opinion on a serve in singles, it is equally poor form to ask your partner his opinion in doubles. If he is receiving, it is your call and yours alone. When you are receiving it is his call and his alone. Accept his call without question. Should he ask your advice, the best answer is a pleasant "I defer to you" or "Please make the call." Under no circumstances volunteer a call on a serve you or your partner has made to the opposite court. No matter how certain you are about where the serve went, let the decision be made on the other side without your help. Bite your tongue if necessary to keep quiet, but keep quiet. If they ask your advice, do not give it. The answer again is "I defer to you." If a serve you are sure went out is returned as a good ball, play it as a good ball. Do not stop in your tracks and ask: "Was that good?" You deserve to lose the point if you do.

Much of what has been said relative to calling bad serves applies to calling other strokes out. In singles, it is your responsibility to call the balls on your side of the net. In doubles, it is yours and/or your partner's, depending upon which one of you saw the ball. If you are in doubt, or if you and your partner disagree, don't get into a debate. Call the ball good. Always give your opponent the benefit of the doubt in a close call, and avoid postmortems. Uncertain calls, late calls and debated calls are as taboo on ground strokes as on serves.

Always make sure that your opponent is ready to receive your serve before you serve. This applies to the second as well as to the first serve. It is not necessary to ask if he is ready but it is polite to look directly at him before beginning your serve so that you can decide for yourself if he is. If you see that he is still walking back into position, or fending off a bee with his racket or diverting an errant ball from rolling into the court, wait. If you are on the receiving end of a serve made before you are ready, it is perfectly proper to call "Not ready" and refuse the serve. Many players, particularly new ones, don't do this either because they do not know they have a right to, or because they are too embarrassed to admit they were not ready. Do not be. Stand your ground and refuse, pleasantly, to play the ball. It is the fastest way to cure a fast server.

The server who deliberately stalls, dragging out each service interminably, is another problem. He gets into position, then bounces the ball eight or ten times, then looks up and around and across the adjacent courts before actually tossing the ball. By the time it finally leaves his racket you are exhausted just from watching it. A bounce or two, a couple of deep breaths, a momentary pause to steady the nerves before serving are all reasonable. The same applies between games and in changing courts. A brief stop to wipe brow or glasses is fine, but long drawn-out delays, constant foot dragging, ball kicking, towel rubbing and shoe tying border dangerously on delaying tactics. Overdoing any of them rarely wins friends or influences people.

There is a difference, however, between a deliberate service stall and repeating a bad toss. Unless your opponent is so much better than you that he never makes a bad toss (which puts him up there with the gods) and therefore cannot understand anyone else doing so, he will be sympathetic to your problem. A bad toss is almost inevitably a bad serve, and there is no real fun in

winning a game on the other fellow's double-faults. Toss the ball until it is in the right position to hit properly, even if this means three or four tosses. Obviously you will not need this many tosses on every serve (if you do, you need some service practice), but when you do, take them. Do not let an impatient opponent psych you into swinging at a hopeless target. Do not use the toss as a stall but do not give up your option to retoss when it is necessary.

Avoid foot-faulting. Although foot-faulting is the most flagrant abuse in weekend tennis, it is one for which there is no justification. Club players at every level are guilty of it, women and men equally. It is a careless, sloppy, thoroughly illegal error that is not tolerated in tournament play but is overlooked in as much as 90 percent of weekend play. There is no point in incurring the ire of your friends by calling foot-faults in friendly games, but you can concentrate on not foot-faulting yourself. Make it an unbreakable rule and, who knows, you may set an example for some of the regular violators.

Be magnanimous whenever you are on the court. Besides giving your opponent the benefit of a close call, pleasantly and graciously, give him an opportunity to make an extra serve if he is interrupted or distracted by conditions beyond his control. If he has faulted on his first serve and is delayed in making his second because of an errant ball from another court, or an elaborate return of his faulted ball or for any reason that forces him to lose his timing and concentration, the polite reaction from you is to say: "Serve again, please" or "Take two." Be gracious. It is the best attitude at all levels of tennis.

So, too, is being honest. It is difficult

to believe that anyone would cheat deliberately at tennis, but unfortunately some people do. There are people who steal from church poor boxes, who pad expense accounts, who overcharge their neighbors too, but they are almost always people you do not know. It is a shock to find that someone you have known for years, someone whose integrity you considered above reproach, cheats at a game. A game, after all, is sport, and the very essence of sport is honesty.

Certainly you should give any player the benefit of the doubt before deciding that his behavior is out-and-out cheating. Assume that his mistakes are honest whenever possible, but if they are persistent—if, for example, he regularly calls balls out that are clearly in—short of employing linesmen to take over the calls, the best solution is not to play with him at all. A habitual cheater will soon be ostracized from any group. It is just a matter of time. The inadvertent cheater is a more difficult case because he may not actually realize his transgressions. Some players are so strongly motivated to win that they are actually blinded (in their favor) by aggressiveness. They genuinely see your ball miss the tape when in actuality it caught a piece of it. You might suggest that they read this chapter, and if it does not ring any bells for them and they continue to call everything in their own favor, you will do them and yourself a favor by not being available the next time they suggest a game.

It does not hurt to review your own behavior when it comes to close calls. In a refereeless situation, particularly when the game is fast, anyone can make a mistake. But if your partner is beginning to look more and more pained

by your calls, double check that you are not suffering from winner blindness yourself. Remember, when in doubt, call in your opponent's favor. At the very least, suggest replaying the point. Remember, too, that if you hit a ball that is out, it is no longer considered to be out but is in play. If you fail to get it back, too bad. You cannot hit it and then call it out. Nor should you catch a ball that is obviously out before letting it bounce first. Most clubs do not enforce this rule in normal play, but many do in tournaments. Whether it is enforced or not, it is discourteous to your opponent to catch an out ball.

Another area in which you must be scrupulous is in calling your own errors when a referee is not present. If you hit the ball on a double-bounce, hit the net with the racket, hit a volley before it has cleared the net on your side or carry the ball (these are the most common examples), it is your responsibility to stop play and to call out the error to your opponent. It is poor form for him to call your errors in such a situation, but worse form for you to force him into doing so.

Keep conversations on the court to a minimum. In women's weekend tennis, that is like saying keep your mink in the closet all year round. But while women are the prime offenders in this area, they are not the only ones. One of the worst jabberwockies at Gipsy Trail is a man. He mumbles, grumbles, dissects each play, postmortems each point, asks endless questions and verbally interrupts play most of the time. As a generalization, however, women are pretty bad about keeping their mouths closed during play. How gabby they are seems to relate directly to their level of skill. Really top women players are as silent as sphinxes, speaking only when absolutely necessary on the courts, and then sparingly. Poor women players, on the other hand, carry on a steady stream of conversation which suggests something about their ability to concentrate. If you review the chapter on strategy, you will note how much emphasis is placed on focusing eye and mind totally upon the ball to the exclusion of all else. If your mind is on the latest bit of gossip, it cannot possibly be on the ball. If you really want to talk, stay off the courts. Nothing is more maddening or distracting to another player than being bombarded with silly chatter all afternoon, whether on his own court or an adjacent one. It is bad manners, bad tennis and bad news.

This does not mean that you must never open your mouth on the court. It simply means you do not let it remain open. Besides announcing the score when serving and making the calls for which you are responsible, it is often necessary and practical to communicate verbally with your partner in doubles. When a shot comes down the middle of the court, for example, it is always a good idea to call "Mine" or "Yours" so that you do not both wind up staring at the ball as it goes by, or worse still, cracking your heads together as you simultaneously try for it. If you are running for a lob you can reach, let her know. If you wind up on her side of the court, shout "Switch" or "Change" so she can cover the part of the court you have left unprotected.

Besides such functional doubles calls, you should by all means commend a really spectacular shot made either by your opponent or your partner. This does not mean that you give a long-winded speech but that you acknowl-edge an excellent performance with the words "Good shot" or "Nice serve." This, too, can be carried to such extremes that it becomes gamesmanship rather than good sportsmanship. Effusive flattery and excessive compliments are in bad taste because they are usually perceived as deliberate ploys to rattle your opponent. If his performance is all that magnificent, save the praise for after the game, when you will be applauded as a good loser.

Although women are more often guilty of chitchat during play, men are the real villains when it comes to beating themselves verbally. The man who berates his strokes, complains about his every error, corrects his form audibly and who swears, shouts and generally performs like a juvenile in a temper tantrum is a nuisance to everyone. He is the type of fellow who throws his racket on the ground after a bad shot or who slams it at the net every time he changes courts. Even when he is winning, he complains and gripes and gesticulates as if his partner were committing some felony against him. If he is unattractive when winning, he is impossible when losing.

Whether you win or lose, you should always end a match with a handshake and a word of praise for your opponent. Try, if you are a winner, to get to the net first, hand outstretched, with a smile and a "Good match." If you cleaned your opponent 6–0, 6–0, don't overdo the praise since he obviously will not believe you. On the other hand, it is bad form to rub in your victory with comments such as "Boy, I really wiped the court with you." Nor will he appreciate a lesson in what he did wrong, or worse still, after having cleaned him, a postmortem on what *you* did wrong. It is one thing to beat an opponent badly and another to then imply that you should have been able to do so with both ankles tied together and playing with the wrong hand.

If you are the loser, it is just as important to shake hands, smile and comment graciously on the match. (A word of caution: Do not attempt to jump over the net unless you are sure you can clear it.) "That was well played" or "A good job" are adequate congratulations. You do not have to give a testimonial. Nor should you offer profuse explanations for your own performance. Lengthy diatribes about your own deficiencies or debilities are seldom welcome. If you were really that weak or that sick, you should not have played at all. If you want to make sure that you do not play again, make comments such as "You really know how to pull them out of a hat," "It certainly helps to make your own calls," "My grandmother could have done a better job in a coma," or a barely audible "Dirty rotten cheat." Even if you hate your opponent, leave the court with him, looking friendly.

There is no substitute for being pleasant on the courts. The player who is well mannered, who is gracious and who smiles will have many invitations to play even if he is not the most talented player around. In spite of the blue-ribbon bulldogs and the snappy terriers, it is the friendly, even-tempered retriever who wins the real ribbons. One of the most popular players at Gipsy Trail is far from being at the top of the ladder (if we could ever get a ladder started), but she is in such demand as a partner both in singles and doubles that she could play eight hours a day if she chose. She always arrives at the court on time, with tennis balls, a towel, a big thermos of iced tea or ice water to share with the others, a smile on her face and a pleasant, cheery greeting for all. Winning or losing, her manner and her manners never change. She is always a lady, a sportswoman and a champion regardless of how the score comes out. About the only complaint that can be made about her is that she also plays golf so she is not on the courts as often as everyone would like her to be. But the image she leaves there is untarnishable.

Some people are pleasant to everyone else but their spouses. There is an old and time-worn gag that goes: "Why marry your mixed doubles partner? Isn't marriage tough enough without that?" Maybe the joke should be: "Isn't marriage tough enough without playing mixed doubles?" Whatever the form, some married couples simply should not play together. They may be polite, courteous and well mannered to their opponents and other partners, but when they get in a mixed doubles game with their mates, they become rude, overbearing and insulting. A man who would not dream of instructing anyone else, male or female, on the courts will criticize, correct and dissect his wife's strokes as if he were running a tennis clinic. He will groan at her errors, practically knock her down to poach a ball from under her feet, shake his head and stamp his feet at every lost point, and blame all losses on her while taking full credit for all wins. This man obviously should not play tennis with his wife. Marital hostilities are best confined to home; they are an embarrassment and a nuisance to others on the courts. If playing with your spouse is torture instead of fun for either of you, find another tennis partner and save your mate for better things. The popular woman mentioned earlier and her husband came to this conclusion years ago and it doubtless accounts for their mutual equanimity. On their wedding day, she recalls, as they walked down the aisle after the ceremony, her new groom turned to her and said: "Just think, this means I shall never have to play tennis with you again." He has not, and they *have* lived happily ever after.

If you are lucky enough to marry or to be married to someone who enjoys tennis as much as you, who complements your game and who really likes to play with you, do not treat the situation lightly. You are thrice blessed because you both have a sport you can share and grow old with together. It is one you can take with you on vacations and business trips, and relax with after work and on weekends. It will keep you both young, active and enriched for the rest of your lives.

If you have never played tennis, now is the time to learn. Millions of people like you are doing just that, and they are discovering to their delight that age and athletic ability have little to do with the genuine pleasure of the sport. It offers something for everyone. After all, it is a game I have learned not only to play but to love.

XVI. Rules of Lawn Tennis

The author is grateful to the United States Lawn Tennis Assocation for permission to reprint the following official code of rules along with explanation, examples and comments as prepared by the USLTA Tennis Umpires Association.

THE SINGLES GAME

RULE 1

Dimensions and Equipment

The Court shall be a rectangle, 78 feet long and 27 feet wide. It shall be divided across the middle by a net, suspended from a cord or metal cable of a maximum diameter of one-third of an inch, the ends of which shall be attached to, or pass over, the tops of two posts, 3 feet 6 inches high, the center of which shall be 3 feet outside the Court on each side. The height of the net shall be 3 feet at the center, where it shall be held down taut by a strap not more than 2 inches wide. There shall be a band covering the cord or metal cable and the top of the net not less than 2 inches nor more than 2½ inches in depth on each side. The lines bounding the ends and sides of the Court shall respectively be called the Baselines and the Side-lines. On each side of the net, at a distance of 21 feet from it and parallel with it, shall be drawn the Service-lines. The space on each side of the net between the service-line and the side-lines shall be divided into two equal parts called the service-courts by the center service-line,

which must be 2 inches in width, drawn half-way between, and parallel with, the side-lines. Each base-line shall be bisected by an imaginary continuation of the center service-line to a line 4 inches in length and 2 inches in width called the center mark drawn inside the Court, at right angles to and in contact with such base-lines. All other lines shall not be less than 1 inch nor more than 2 inches in width, except the base-line, which may be 4 inches in width, and all measurements shall be made to the outside of the lines.

Note.—In the case of the International Lawn Tennis Championship (Davis Cup) or other Official Championships of the International Federation, there shall be a space behind each base-line of not less than 21 feet and at the sides of not less than 12 feet.

EXPLANATION OF RULE 1

The center of the posts in doubles should be 3 feet outside the doubles court.

The net should be 33 feet wide for a singles court, and 42 feet wide for a doubles court. It should touch the ground along its entire length and come flush to the posts at all points.

It is important to have a stick 3 feet, 6 inches long, with a notch cut in at the 3-foot mark for the purpose of measuring the height of the net at the posts and in the center. These measurements, as well as the measurements of the court itself, always should be made before starting to play an important match.

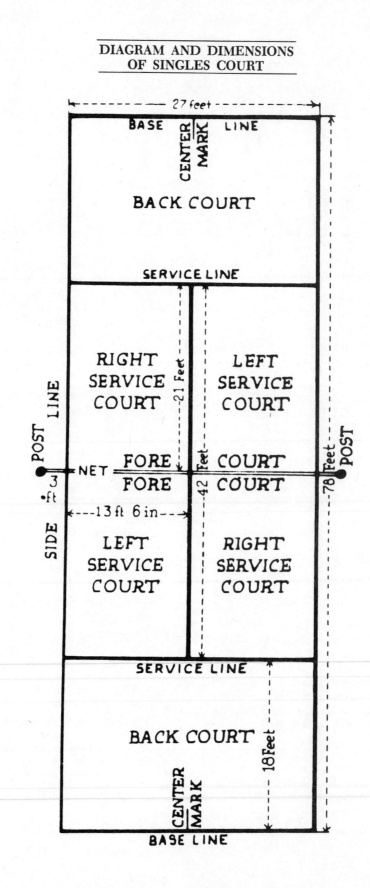

RULE 2

Permanent Fixtures

The permanent fixtures of the Court shall include not only the net, posts, cord or metal cable, strap and band, but also, where there are any such, the back and side stops, the stands, fixed or movable seats and chairs around the Court, and their occupants, all other fixtures around and above the Court, and the Umpire, Net-cord Judge, Foot-fault Judge, Linesmen and Ball Boys when in their respective places.

RULE 3

Ball—Size, Weight and Bound

The ball shall have a uniform outer surface and may be white or yellow in color. If there are any seams they shall be stitchless. The ball shall be more than two and a half inches and less than two and five-eighths inches in diameter, and more than two ounces and less than two and one-sixteenth ounces in weight. The ball shall have a bound of more than 53 inches and less than 58 inches when dropped 100 inches upon a concrete base. The ball shall have a forward deformation of more than .230 of an inch and less than .290 of an inch and a return deformation of more than .355 of an inch and less than .425 of an inch at 18 lb. load. The two deformation figures shall be the average of three individual readings along three axes of the ball and no two individual readings shall differ by more than .030 of an inch in each case. All tests for bound, size and deformation shall be made in accordance with the Regulations in the Appendix hereto.

Note.—At the Annual General Meeting of the I.L.T.F. held on 12th July, 1967, it was agreed that for the time being non-pressurized balls and low-pressure balls may not be used in the International Lawn Tennis Championship (Davis Cup), unless mutually agreed by the two nations taking part in any particular event.

NOTE

"How often may the player have new balls?"

Generally the ball-change pattern is specified by the Referee before the match is started. According to Tournament Regulation 14 (g) the Umpire, subject to the approval of the Referee, may decide when new balls are required to insure fairness of playing conditions. In matches where there is no Umpire, the players should agree beforehand on this matter.

RULE 4

Server and Receiver

The Players shall stand on opposite sides of the net; the player who first delivers the ball shall be called the Server, and the other the Receiver.

Case 1. Does a player, attempting a stroke, lose the point if he crosses an imaginary line in the extension of the net, (a) before striking the ball (b) after striking the ball?

Decision. He does not lose the point in either case by crossing the imaginary line provided he does not enter the lines bounding his opponent's court. (Rule 18 (e).) In regard to hindrance, his opponent may ask for the decision of the umpire under Rules 19 and 23.

Case 2. The Server claims that the Receiver must stand within the lines bounding his court. Is this necessary?

Decision. No. The Receiver may stand wherever he pleases on his own side of the net.

RULE 5

Choice of Sides and Service

The choice of sides and the right to be Server or Receiver in the first game shall be decided by toss. The player winning the toss may choose, or require his opponent to choose:

(a) The right to be Server or Receiver, in which case the other player shall choose the side; or

(b) The side, in which case the other player shall choose the right to be Server or Receiver.

RULE 6

Delivery of Service

The service shall be delivered in the following manner. Immediately before commencing to serve, the Server shall stand with both feet at rest behind (i.e. farther from the net than) the base-line, and within the imaginary continuations of the center-mark and side-line. The Server shall then project the ball by hand into the air in any direction and before it hits the ground strike it with his racket, and the delivery shall be deemed to have been completed at the moment of the impact of the racket and the ball. A player with the use of only one arm may utilize his racket for the projection.

Case 1. May the Server in a singles game take his stand behind the portion of the base-line between the sidelines of the singles court and the doubles court?

Decision. No.

Case 2. If a player, when serving, throws up two or more balls instead of one, does he lose that service?

Decision. No. A let should be called, but if the umpire regards the action as deliberate he may take action under Rule 19.

Case 3. May a player serve underhand?

Decision. Yes. There is no restriction regarding the kind of service which may be used; that is, the player may use an underhand or overhand service at his discretion.

RULE 7

Foot Fault

The Server shall throughout the delivery of the service:

(a) Not change his position by walking or running.

(b) Not touch, with either foot, any area other than that behind the base-line within the imaginary extension of the center-mark and side-line.

Note.—The following interpretation of Rule 7 was approved by the International Federation on 9th July 1958:—

(a) The Server shall not, by slight movements of the feet which do not materially affect the location originally taken up by him, be deemed "to change his position by walking or running."

(b) The word "foot" means the extremity of the leg below the ankle.

COMMENT: This rule covers the most decisive stroke in the game, and there is no justification for its not being obeyed by players and enforced by officials. No tournament chairman has the right to request or attempt to instruct linesmen and/or umpires to disregard violations of it.

RULE 8

From Alternate Courts

(a) In delivering the service, the Server shall stand alternately behind the right and left Courts, beginning from the right in every game. If service from a wrong half of the Court occurs and is undetected, all play resulting from such wrong service or services shall stand, but the inaccuracy of the station shall be corrected immediately it is discovered.

(b) The ball served shall pass over the net and hit the ground within the Service Court which is diagonally opposite, or upon any line bounding such Court, before the Receiver returns it.

COMMENT: The Receiver is not allowed to volley a served ball; i.e., he must allow it to strike in his court first. (See Rule 16 (a).)

EXPLANATION: In matches played without umpire or linesmen, it is customary for the Receiver to determine whether the service is good or a fault; indeed, each player makes the calls for all balls hit to his side of the net. (In doubles, the Receiver's partner makes the calls with respect to the service line.)

RULE 9

Faults

The Service is a fault:

(a) If the Server commit any breach of Rules 6, 7 or 8;

(b) If he miss the ball in attempting to strike it;

(c) If the ball served touch a permanent fixture (other than the net, strap or band) before it hits the ground.

Case 1. After throwing a ball up preparatory to serving, the Server decides not to strike at it and catches it instead. Is it a fault?

Decision. No.

Case 2. In serving in a singles game played on a doubles court with doubles and singles net posts, the ball hits a singles post and then hits the ground within the lines of the correct service court. Is this a fault or a let?

Decision. In serving it is a fault because the singles post, the doubles post, and that portion of the net, strap or band between them are permanent fixtures. (Rules 2 and 9, and note to Rule 22.)

EXPLANATION: *The significant point governing Case 2 is that the part of the net and band "outside" the singles sticks is not part of the net over which this singles match is being played. Thus such a serve is a fault under the provisions of article (c) above . . . By the same token, this would be a fault also if it were a singles game played with permanent posts in the singles position. (See Case 1 under Rule 22 for difference between "service" and "good return" with respect to a ball's hitting a net post.)*

COMMENT: *In doubles, if the Server's delivery hits his partner, the serve is a fault (not necessarily loss of point). See Rule 37.*

RULE 10

Service After a Fault

After a fault (if it be the first fault) the Server shall serve again from behind the same half of the Court from which he served that fault, unless the service was from the wrong half, when, in accordance with Rule 8, the Server shall be entitled to one service only from behind the other half. A fault may not be claimed after the next service has been delivered.

Case 1. A player serves from a wrong court. He loses the point and then claims it was a fault because of his wrong station.

Decision. The point stands as played and the next service should be from the correct station according to the score.

Case 2. The point score being 15 all, the Server, by mistake, serves from the left-hand court. He wins the point. He then serves again from the right-hand court, delivering a fault. The mistake in station is then discovered. Is he entitled to the previous point? From which court should he next serve?

Decision. The previous point stands.

The next service should be from the left-hand court, the score being 30/15, and the Server has served one fault.

RULE 11

Receiver Must Be Ready

The Server shall not serve until the Receiver is ready. If the latter attempt to return the service, he shall be deemed ready. If, however, the Receiver signify that he is not ready, he may not claim a fault because the ball does not hit the ground within the limits fixed for the service.

EXPLANATION OF RULE 11

The Server must wait until the Receiver is ready for the second service as well as the first, and if the Receiver claims to be not ready and does not make any effort to return a service, the Server may not claim the point, even though the service was good.

RULE 12

A Let

In all cases where a let has to be called under the rules, or to provide for an interruption to play, it shall have the following interpretations:

(a) When called solely in respect of a service, that one service only shall be replayed.

(b) When called under any other circumstance, the point shall be replayed.

Case 1. A service is interrupted by some cause outside those defined in Rule 13. Should the service only be re-played?

Decision. No. the whole point must be replayed.

EXPLANATION: *The phrase "in respect of a service" in (a) means a let because a served ball has touched the net before landing in the proper court. OR because the Receiver was not ready . . . Case 1 refers to a second serve, and the decision means that if the interruption occurs during delivery of the second service, the Server gets two serves.*

EXAMPLE: *On a second service a Linesman calls "fault" and immediately corrects it (the Receiver meanwhile having let the ball go by.) The Server is entitled to two serves, on this ground: The corrected call means that*

153

the Server had put the ball into play with a good serve, and once the ball is in play and a let is called, the point must be replayed . . . Note, however, that if the serve were an unmistakable one—that is, the Umpire was sure the erroneous call had no part in the Receiver's inability to play the ball—the point should be declared for the Server.

Case 2. If a ball in play becomes broken, should a let be called?

Decision. Yes.

Note.—The USLTA Umpires Committee has authorized this interpretation. A ball shall be regarded as having become "broken" if, in the opinion of the Umpire, it is found to have lost compression to the point of being unfit for further play, or unfit for any reason, and there is any likelihood that this deficiency had an effect on the preceding point.

RULE 13

The service is a let

The service is a let:

(a) If the ball served touch the net, strap or band, and is otherwise good, or, after touching the net, strap or band, touch the Receiver or anything which he wears or carries before hitting the ground.

(b) If a service or a fault be delivered when the Receiver is not ready (see Rule 11).

COMMENT: A "let" called for the reason the Receiver had indicated he is not ready, if called on second service, does not annul a fault on first serve.

RULE 14

When Receiver Becomes Server

At the end of the first game the Receiver shall become the Server, and the Server Receiver; and so on alternately in all the subsequent games of a match. If a player serve out of turn, the player who ought to have served shall serve as soon as the mistake is discovered, but all points scored before such discovery shall be reckoned. If a game shall have been completed before such discovery, the order of service remains as altered. A fault served before such discovery shall not be reckoned.

RULE 15

Ball in Play Till Point Decided

A ball is in play from the moment at which it is delivered in service. Unless a fault or a let be called, it remains in play until the point is decided.

COMMENT: A point is not "decided" simply when, or because, a good shot has clearly passed a player, nor when an apparently bad shot passes over a baseline or sideline. An outgoing ball is still definitely "in play" until it actually strikes the ground, backstop or other fixture. The same applies to a good ball, bounding after it has landed in the proper court. A ball that becomes imbedded in the net is out of play.

Case 1. A ball is played into the net; the player on the other side, thinking that the ball is coming over, strikes at it and hits the net. Who loses the point?

Decision. If the player touched the net while the ball was still in play, he loses the point.

RULE 16

Server Wins Point

The Server wins the point:

(a) If the ball served, not being a let under Rule 13, touch the Receiver or anything he wears or carries, before it hits the ground;

(b) If the Receiver otherwise loses the point as provided by Rule 18.

RULE 17

Receiver Wins Point

The Receiver wins the point:

(a) If the Server serve two consecutive faults;

(b) If the Server otherwise lose the point as provided by Rule 18.

RULE 18

Player Loses Point

A player loses the point if:

(a) He fail, before the ball in play has hit the ground twice consecutively, to return it directly over the net (except as provided in Rule 22(a) or (c)); or

(b) He return the ball in play so that it hits the ground, a permanent fixture, or other object, outside any of the lines which bound his opponent's Court (except as provided in Rule 22 (a) and (c)); or

(c) He volley the ball and fail to make a good return even when standing outside the Court; or

(d) He touch or strike the ball in play with his racket more than once in making a stroke; or

(e) He or his racket (in his hand or otherwise) or anything he wears or carries touch the net, posts, cord or metal cable, strap or band, or the ground within his opponent's Court at any time while the ball is in play; or

(f) He volley the ball before it has passed the net; or

(g) The ball in play touch him or anything that he wears or carries, except his racket in his hand or hands; or

(h) He throws his racket at and hits the ball.

EXPLANATION: Referring to (d), a player may be deemed to have "touched the ball more than once" if the ball rests on his racket in such a way that the effect is more that of a "sling" or "throw" than a hit. (See "carry" and "double hit" in Glossary.)

In (g), note that this loss of point occurs regardless of whether the player is inside or outside the bounds of his court when the ball touches him.

Case 1. In delivering a first service which falls outside the proper court, the Server's racket slips out of his hand and flies into the net. Does he lose the point?

Decision. If his racket touches the net while the ball is in play, the Server loses the point. (Rule 18 (e).)

Case 2. In serving, the racket flies from the Server's hand and touches the net before the ball has touched the ground. Is this a fault, or does the player lose the point?

Decision. The Server loses the point because his racket touches the net while the ball is in play. (Rule 18 (e).)

Case 3. A and B are playing against C and D. A is serving to D. C touches the net before the ball touches the ground. A fault is then called because the service falls outside the service court. Do C and D lose the point?

Decision. The call "fault" is an erroneous one. C and D have already lost the point before "fault" could be called, because C touched the net while the ball was in play. (Rule 18 (e).)

Case 4. May a player jump over the net into his opponent's court while the ball is in play and not suffer penalty?

Decision. No; he loses the point. (Rule 18 (e).)

Case 5. A cuts the ball just over the net, and it returns to A's side. B, unable to reach the ball, throws his racket and hits the ball. Both racket and ball fall over the net on A's court. A returns the ball outside of B's court. Does B win or lose the point?

Decision. B loses the point. (Rule 18 (e) and (h).)

Case 6. A player standing outside the service court is struck by the service ball before it has touched the ground. Does he win or lose the point?

Decision. The player struck loses the point (Rule 18 (g), except as provided under Rule 13 (a).)

Case 7. A player standing outside the court volleys the ball or catches it in his hand and claims the point because the ball was certainly going out of court.

Decision. In no circumstance can he claim the point;

(1) If he catches the ball he loses the point under Rule 18 (g).

(2) If he volleys it and makes a bad return he loses the point under Rule 18 (c).

(3) If he volleys it and makes a good return, the rally continues.

EXPLANATION: In Case 6 above, the exception referred to is that of a served ball that has touched the net en route into the Receiver's court; in that circumstance it is a let service, not loss of point. Such a let does not annul a previous (first service) fault; therefore if it occurs on second service, the Server has one serve coming.

EXAMPLE: Player has let racket go out of his hand clearly before racket hits ball, but the ball rebounds from his racket into proper court. This is not a good return; player loses point under Rule 18 (h).

COMMENT: The strokes referred to in (d) of Rule 18 are difficult to define and to rule on. Some are obvious, others are arguable. Most experienced umpires give the player the benefit of the doubt, but do call it a double-hit if there is even the suggestion of a "second push" or, as noted in the explanatory note for (d), the return seems to be more of a sling than a hit.

RULE 19

Player Hinders Opponent

If a player commits any act either deliberate or involuntary which, in the opinion of the Umpire, hinders his opponent in making a stroke, the Umpire shall in the first case award the point to the opponent, and in the second case order the point to be replayed.

Case 1. Is a player liable to a penalty if in making a stroke he touches his opponent?

Decision. No, unless the Umpire deems it necessary to take action under Rule 19.

Case 2. When a ball bounds back over the net, the player concerned may reach over the net in order to play the ball. What is the ruling if the player is hindered from doing this by his opponent?

Decision. In accordance with Rule 19, the Umpire may either award the point to the player hindered, or order the point to be replayed. (See also Rule 23.)

RULE 20

Ball Falling on Line—Good

A ball falling on a line is regarded as falling in the Court bounded by that line.

COMMENT: In matches played without umpire or linesmen, it is customary for each player to make the calls on all balls hit to his side of the net.

RULE 21

Ball Touching Permanent Fixture

If the ball in play touch a permanent fixture (other than the net, posts, cord or metal cable, strap or band) after it has hit the ground, the player who struck it wins the point; if before it hits the ground his opponent wins the point.

Case 1. A return hits the Umpire or his chair or stand. The player claims that the ball was going into court.

Decision. He loses the point.

RULE 22

Good Return

It is a good return:

(a) If the ball touch the net, posts, cord or metal cable, strap or band, provided that it passes over any of them and hits the ground within the Court; or

(b) If the ball, served or returned, hit the ground within the proper Court and rebound or be blown back over the net, and the player whose turn it is to strike reach over the net and play the ball, provided that neither he nor any part of his clothes or racket touch the net, posts, cord or metal cable, strap or band or the ground within his opponent's Court, and that the stroke be otherwise good; or

(c) If the ball be returned outside the post, either above or below the level of the top of the net, even though it touch the post, provided that it hits the ground within the proper Court; or

(d) If a player's racket pass over the net after he has returned the ball, provided the ball pass the net before being played and be properly returned; or

(e) If a player succeeded in returning the ball, served or in play, which strikes a ball lying in the Court.

Note.—If, for the sake of convenience, a doubles court be equipped with singles posts for the purpose of singles game, then the doubles posts and those portions of the net, cord or metal cable and band outside such singles posts shall be regarded as "permanent fixtures *other than* net, post, strap or band," and therefore *not* posts or parts of the net of that singles game.

A return that passes under the net cord between the singles and adjacent doubles post without touching either net cord, net or doubles post and falls within the area of play, is a good return. (But in doubles this would be a "through"—loss of point.)

Case 1. A ball going out of court hits a net post and falls within the lines of the opponent's court. Is the stroke good?

Decision. If a service; no, under Rule 9 (c). If other than a service; yes, under Rule 22 (a).

Case 2. Is it a good return if a player returns the ball holding his racket in both hands?

Decision. Yes.

Case 3. The Service, or ball in play, strikes a ball lying in the court. Is the point won or lost thereby?

Decision. No. Play must continue. If it is not clear to the Umpire that the right ball is returned a let should be called.

Case 4. May a player use more than one racket at any time during play?

Decision. No: the whole implication of the rules is singular.

Case 5. May a player request that a ball or balls lying in his opponent's court be removed?

Decision. Yes, but not while a ball is in play.

RULE 23

Interference

In case a player is hindered in making a stroke by anything not within his control except a permanent fixture of the Court, or except as provided for in Rule 19, the point shall be replayed.

Case 1. A spectator gets into the way of a player, who fails to return the ball. May the player then claim a let?

Decision. Yes, if in the Umpire's decision he was obstructed by circumstances beyond his control, but not if due to permanent fixtures of the Court or the arrangements of the ground.

Case 2. A player is interfered with as in Case No. 1, and the Umpire calls a let. The Server had previously served a fault. Has he the right to two services?

Decision. Yes; as the ball is in play, the point, not merely the stroke, must be replayed as the rule provides.

Case 3. May a player claim a let under Rule 23 because he thought his opponent was being hindered, and consequently did not expect the ball to be returned?

Decision. No.

Case 4. Is a stroke good when a ball in play hits another ball in the air?

Decision. A let should be called unless the other ball is in the air by the act of one of the players, in which case the Umpire will decide under Rule 19.

Case 5. If an Umpire or other judge erroneously calls "fault" or "out" and then corrects himself, which of the calls shall prevail?

Decision. A let must be called, unless, in the opinion of the Umpire, neither player is hindered in his game, in which case the corrected call shall prevail.

Case 6. If the first ball served—a fault—rebounds, interfering with the Receiver at the time of the second service, may the Receiver claim a let?

Decision. Yes. But if he had an opportunity to remove the ball from the court and negligently failed to do so, he may not claim a let.

Case 7. Is it a good stroke if the ball touches a stationary or moving object on the court?

Decision. It is a good stroke unless the stationary object came into court after the ball was put into play in which case a "let" must be called. If the ball in play strikes an object moving along or above the surface of the court a "let" must be called.

Case 8. What is the ruling if the first service is a fault, the second service correct, and it becomes necessary to call a let under the provision of Rule 23 or if the Umpire is unable to decide the point?

Decision. The fault shall be annulled and the whole point replayed.

COMMENT: See Rule 12 and Explanation thereto.

RULE 24

The Game

If a player wins his first point, the score is called *15* for that player; on winning his second point, the score is called *30* for that player; on winning his third point, the score is called *40* for that player, and the fourth point won by a player is scored *game* for that player except as below:

If both players have won three points, the score is called *deuce;* and the next point won by a player is called *advantage* for that player. If the same player wins the next point, he wins the game; if the other player wins the next point the score is again called *deuce;* and so on until a player wins the two points immediately following the score at deuce, when the game is scored for that player.

COMMENT: In matches played without an umpire the Server should announce, in a voice audible to his opponent and spectators, the set score at the beginning of each game, and (audible at least to his opponent) point scores as the game goes on. Misunderstandings will be averted if this practice is followed.

RULE 25

The Set

A player (or players) who first wins six games wins a set; except that he must win by a margin of two games over his opponent and where necessary a set shall be extended until this margin be achieved. (Note: See Tie-breakers)

RULE 26

When Players Change Sides

The players shall change sides at the end of the first, third and every subsequent alternate game of each set, and at the end of each set unless the total number of games in such set be even, in which case the change is not made until the end of the first game of the next set.

RULE 27

Maximum Number of Sets

The maximum number of sets in a match shall be 5, or, where women take part, 3.

RULE 28

Rules Apply to Both Sexes

Except where otherwise stated, every reference in these Rules to the masculine includes the feminine gender.

RULE 29

Decisions of Umpire and Referee

In matches where an Umpire is appointed, his decision shall be final; but where a Referee is appointed, an appeal shall lie to him from the decision of an Umpire on a question of law, and in all such cases the decision of the Referee shall be final, except that in Davis Cup matches the decision of a linesman can be changed by the Referee, or by the Umpire with the consent of the Referee.

The Referee, in his discretion, may at any time postpone a match on account of darkness or the condition of the ground or the weather. In any case of postponement the previous score and previous occupancy of Courts shall hold good, unless the Referee and the players unanimously agree otherwise.

RULE 30

Play shall be continuous from the first service till the match be concluded; provided that after the third set or when women take part, the second set, either player is entitled to a rest, which shall not exceed 10 minutes, or in countries situated between Latitude 15 degrees North and Latitude 15 degrees South, 45 minutes, and provided further that when necessitated by circumstances not within the control of the players, the Umpire may suspend play for such a period as he may consider necessary. If play be suspended and be not resumed until a later day the rest may be taken only after the third set (or when women take part the second set) of play on such later day, completion of an unfinished set being counted as one set. These provisions shall be strictly construed, and play shall never be suspended, delayed or interfered with for the purpose of enabling a player to recover his strength or his wind, or to receive instruction or advice. The Umpire shall be the sole judge of such suspension, delay or interference, and after giving due warning he may disqualify the offender.

EXAMPLE: In a best-of-five-sets match, play is suspended because of darkness at one set all and 2-all in the third. Next day play is resumed, and after Player A wins the third set (10-8) he claims he is entitled to an intermission. He is not. Note that Rule 30 specifies the rest period may come after the third set of play on that day. In cases of prolonged delay, with resumption the same day, it is advisable to come to an agreement about any further rest periods before resuming play.

(a) Any nation is at liberty to modify the first provision of Rule 30, or omit it from its regulations governing tournaments, matches, or competitions held in its own country, other than the International Lawn Tennis Championships (Davis Cup and Federation Cup).

(b) When changing sides a maximum of one minute shall elapse from the cessation of the previous game to the time players are ready to begin the next game.

EXPLANATION: In Men's and Juniors' (males 18) events there is no rest period in a best-of-three-sets match, but in a best-of-five-sets match a 10-minute rest may be taken (must, if either side requests it) after the third set. It may not be taken any time before the third set or at any time after the fourth set has been started. It must be taken after the third set or not at all . . . Likewise, in best-of-three matches where a rest period is allowed, it must be taken after the second set or not at all.

All matches for Juniors shall be the best of three sets WITH NO REST PERIOD, except that in Tennis Center championships or Interscholastic, State and Sectional tournaments equivalent to Tennis Centers, and in National Junior championships, the FINAL ROUND may be best-of-five. If such final requires more than three sets to decide, a rest of 10 minutes after the third set is MANDATORY.

In severe temperature-humidity conditions a Referee may rule that a 10-minute rest may be taken in a Juniors best-of-three-set match. However, to be valid, this must be done before the match is started, and as a matter of the Referee's independent judgment, not in response to a request of a competitor or his coach.

Matches for all players, both boys and girls, in the 16-, 14-, and 12-year classes shall be best-of-three-sets; 10-minute rest before the third set is MANDATORY in *girls 12, 14 and 16, and in boys 12 and 14, OPTIONAL in boys 16. (Optional means at the option of any competitor.)*

NOTE: Use of tiebreakers does not change USLTA regulations regarding rest periods in any age-specified categories. In regular men's and women's divisions a tournament may eliminate rest periods provided advance notice is given.

In Men's 35 and all Seniors' age divisions, and in Father & Son matches, the rest period is optional.

Should a player, on account of physical unfitness or an unavoidable accident, not within his control, be unable to continue play, he must be defaulted.

If an Umpire decides that a player is deliberately stalling to gain time or unfairly disconcert his opponent he should warn the player once, and if the practice continues the Umpire should default him.

Case 1. A player's clothing, footwear, or equipment becomes out of adjustment in such a way that it is impossible or undesirable for him to play on. May play be suspended while the maladjustment is rectified?

> Decision. If this occurs in circumstances not within the control of the player, of which circumstances the Umpire is the sole judge, a suspension may be allowed.

Case 2. If, owing to an accident, a player is unable to continue immediately, is there any limit to the time during which play may be suspended?

> Decision. No allowance may be made for natural loss of physical condition. Consideration may be given by the Umpire for accidental loss of physical ability or condition.

COMMENT: Case 2 refers to an important distinction that should be made between a temporary disability caused by an accident during play, and disability caused by fatigue (cramps, for example). Not even momentary "rest"—other than the normal toweling-off pause at changeover—is allowed for recovery from "natural loss of physical condition."

Case 3. During a doubles game, may one of the partners leave the court while the remaining partner keeps the ball in play?

Decision. Yes, so long as the Umpire is satisfied that play is continuous within the meaning of the rules, and that there is no conflict with Rules 33 and 34.

COMMENT: When a player competes in an event designated as for players of a bracket whose rules as to intermissions and length of match are geared to a different physical status, the player cannot ask for allowances based on his or her age, or her sex. For example, a female competing in an intercollegiate (men's) varsity team match would not be entitled to claim a rest period in a best-of-three-sets match unless that were the condition under which the team competition was normally held.

NOTE: When a match is resumed following an interruption necessitated by weather conditions, it is allowable for the players to engage in a "re-warm-up" period. It may be of the same duration as the warm-up allowed at the start of the match; may be done using the balls that were in play at the time of the interruption, and the time for the next ball change shall not be affected by this.

THE DOUBLES GAME

RULE 31

The above Rules shall apply to the Doubles Game except as below.

RULE 32

Dimension of Court

For the Doubles Game, the Court shall be 36 feet in width, i.e., 4½ feet wider on each side than the Court for the Singles Game, and those portions of the singles side-lines which lie between the two service-lines shall be called the service-side-lines. In other respects, the Court shall be similar to that described in Rule 1, but the portions of the singles side-lines between the baseline and service-line on each side of the net may be omitted if desired.

Case 1. In doubles the Server claims the right to stand at the corner of the court as marked by the doubles side line. Is the foregoing correct or is it necessary that the Server stand within the limits of the center mark and the singles side line?

Decision. The Server has the right to stand anywhere between the center mark and the doubles side lines.

RULE 33

Order of Service

The order of serving shall be decided at the beginning of each set as follows:

The pair who have to serve in the first game of each set shall decide which partner shall do so and the opposing pair shall decide similarly for the second game. The partner of the player who served in the first game shall serve in the third; the partner of the player who served in the second game shall serve in the fourth, and so on in the same order in all the subsequent games of a set.

Case 1. In doubles, one player does not appear in time to play, and his partner claims to be allowed to play single-handed against the opposing players. May he do so?

Decision. No.

EXPLANATION: It is not required that the order of service, as between partners, carry over from one set to the next. Each team is allowed to decide which partner shall serve first for it, in each set. This same option applies with respect to the order of receiving service.

RULE 34

Order of Receiving

The order of receiving the service shall be decided at the beginning of each set as follows:

The pair who have to receive the service in the first game shall decide which partner shall receive the first service, and that partner shall continue to receive the first service in every odd game throughout that set. The opposing pair shall likewise decide which partner shall receive the first service in the second game and that partner shall continue to receive the first service in every even game throughout that set. Partners shall receive the service alternately throughout each game.

EXPLANATION OF RULE 34

The receiving formation of a doubles team may not be changed during a set; only at the start of a new set. Partners must receive throughout each set on the same sides of the court which they originally select when the set begins. The first Server is not required to receive in the right court; he may select either side, but must hold this to the end of the set.

Case 1. Is it allowable in doubles for the Server's partner to stand in a position that obstructs the view of the Receiver?

Decision. Yes. The Server's partner may take any position on his side of the net in or out of the court that he wishes.

RULE 35

Service Out of Turn

If a partner serve out of his turn, the partner who ought to have served shall serve as soon as the mistake is discovered, but all points scored, and any faults served before such discovery shall be reckoned. If a game shall have been completed before such discovery the order of service remains as altered.

RULE 36

Error in Order of Receiving

If during a game the order of receiving the service is changed by the receivers it shall remain as altered until the end of the game in which the mistake is discovered, but the partners shall resume their original order of receiving in the next game of that set in which they are receivers of the service.

RULE 37

Ball Touching Server's Partner Is Fault

The service is a fault as provided for by Rule 9, or if the ball served touch the Server's partner or anything he wears or carries; but if the ball served touch the partner of the Receiver or anything which he wears or carries, not being a let under Rule 13 (a), before it hits the ground, the Server wins the point.

RULE 38

Ball Struck Alternately

The ball shall be struck alternately by one or other player of the opposing pairs, and if a player touches the ball in play with his racket in contravention of this Rule, his opponents win the point.

EXPLANATION: This means that, in the course of making one return, only one member of a doubles team may hit the ball. If both of them hit the ball, either simultaneously or consecutively, it is an illegal return. The partners themselves do not have to "alternate" in making returns. (Mere clashing of rackets does not make a return illegal, if it is clear that only one racket touched the ball.)

DIAGRAM AND DIMENSIONS OF DOUBLES COURT

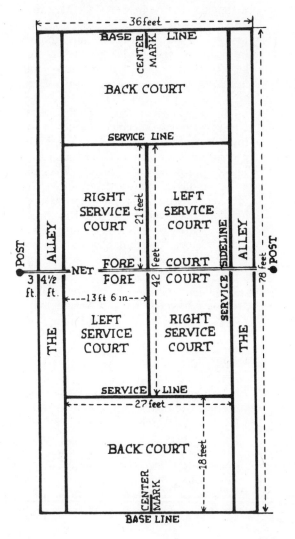

Should any point arise upon which you find it difficult to give a decision or on which you are in doubt as to the proper ruling, immediately write, giving full details, to John Stahr, USLTA Umpires Committee, 65 Briar Cliff Rd., Larchmont, N. Y. 10538, and full instructions and explanations will be sent you.

APPENDIX

Regulations for Making Tests Specified in Rule 3

1. Unless otherwise specified all tests shall be made at a temperature of approximately 68° Fahrenheit (20° Centigrade) and a relative humidity of approximately 60 per cent. All balls should be removed from their container and kept at the recognised temperature and humidity for 24 hours prior to testing, and shall be at that temperature and humidity when the test is commenced.

2. Unless otherwise specified the limits are for a test conducted in an atmospheric pressure resulting in a barometric reading of approximately 30 inches (76 cm.).

3. Other standards may be fixed for localities where the average temperature, humidity or average barometric pressure at which the game is being played differ, materially from 68° Fahrenheit (20° Centigrade), 60 per cent and 30 inches (76 cm.) respectively.

   Applications for such adjusted standards may be made by any National Association to the International Lawn Tennis Federation and if approved shall be adopted for such localities.

4. In all tests for diameter a ring gauge shall be used consisting of a metal plate, preferably non-corrosive of a uniform thickness of one-eighth of an inch (.32cm.) in which there are two circular openings 2.575 inches (6.54 cm.) and 2.700 inches (6.86 cm.) in diameter respectively. The inner surface of the gauge shall have a convex profile with a radius of one-sixteenth of an inch (.16 cm.). The ball shall not drop

through the smaller opening by its own weight and shall drop through the larger opening by its own weight.

5. In all tests for deformation conducted under Rule 3, the machine designed by Percy Herbert Stevens and patented in Great Britain under Patent No. 230250, together with the subsequent additions and improvements thereto, including the modifications required to take return deformations shall be employed or such other machine which is approved by a National Association and gives equivalent readings to the Stevens machine.

6. Procedure for carrying out tests:
   (a) Pre-compression. Before any ball is tested it shall be steadily compressed by approximately one inch (2.54 cm.), on each of three diameters at right angles to one another in succession; this process to be carried out three times (nine compressions in all). All tests to be completed within two hours of pre-compression.
   (b) Bound test (as in Rule 3). Measurements are to be taken from the concrete base to the bottom of the ball.
   (c) Size test (as in paragraph (4) above).
   (d) Weight test (as in Rule 3).
   (e) Deformation test. The ball is placed in position on the modified Stevens machine so that neither platen of the machine is in contact with the cover seam. The contact weight is applied, the pointer and the mark brought level, and the dials set to zero. The test weight equivalent to 18 lb. (8.165 kg.) is placed on the beam and pressure applied by turning the wheel at a uniform speed so that five seconds elapse from the instant the beam leaves its seat until the pointer is brought level with the mark. When turning ceases the reading is recorded (forward deformation). The wheel is turned again until figure ten is reached on the wheel scale (one inch (2.54 cm.) deformation). The wheel is then rotated in the opposite direction at a uniform speed (thus releasing pressure) until the beam pointer again coincides with the mark. After waiting ten seconds the pointer is adjusted to

the mark if necessary. The reading is then recorded (return deformation). This procedure is repeated on each ball across the two diameters at right angles to the initial position and to each other.

RULES OF VASSS 'NO-AD'

(Van Alen Simplified Scoring System)

(All USLTA rules apply except in scoring)

1. The **Advantage Point** is eliminated in the game, and the **Advantage Game** in the Set.

2. The first to win 4 points, 1, 2, 3, 4, (not 15, 30, 40), wins the game, the first to win 6 Games wins the Set. However, where time is a factor, the Set may be reduced from 6 to either 5 or 4 games. If the Score is tied (5 games all) the 9-point Tiebreak decides the Set. (See Tiebreak Rules.) Maximum number of points 79, playing time 25-30 minutes. **It must be emphasized that NO-AD does not improve the handicap problem.**

RULES OF VASSS 'SINGLE POINT'

(All USLTA rules apply except in scoring)

1. It is scored as at Table Tennis—1, 2, 3, 4.

2. The serve changes from A to B every 5 pts. (5, 10, 15). This 5 pt. sequence is called a 'Hand'. Serve changes at the end of the set but not side (N-S). The receiver or team in the fifth point in the hand may choose to receive in right or left court.

3. The first point in each 'Hand' (1, 6, 11, 16, etc.) is served into the Right or Forehand Court.

4. Sides (N-S) are changed on the odd 'Hand', 5 pts. (5, 15, 25).

5. The official set is fixed at 31 points. But where time is at a premium, 21 points may be used.

6. If there is no umpire the Server is re-

quired to **call score loud and clear** after each point.

7. The winner of the set must lead by at least 2 points (31-29). Maximum number of points 69, playing time 25-30 minutes. **SINGLE POINT IS THE KEY TO EFFICIENT HANDICAPPING.** Sudden death decides winner as 30 points all in singles point set.

SUDDEN DEATH 9 POINT TIEBREAK RULES

In the event the score is tied in No-AD at 5 games all or in SINGLE POINT at 30 points all, he who would normally serve the eleventh game in NO-AD or the 61st point in SINGLE POINT shall serve points 1, 2, 5, 6, of the 5 out of 9-point Tiebreak. Sides shall be changed after the first 4 points. The receiver in the tiebreak game shall serve points 3 and 4, 7 and 8, and **if the score shall reach 4 points all, the** 9th point, **which he may serve into either the right or left court.** Each player shall serve 2 points in succession, right-left, 1 and 2, 3 and 4, etc. (See diagram.) At the end of the tiebreak game the **receiver** in the first set (he who served points, 3, 4, 7, 8, 9 of the Tiebreak) shall **commence** serving in the second set. In the event the score is again tied in the second set, 5 games all, or 30 points all respectively, he shall serve points 1, 2, and 5, 6 of the tiebreak game, etc., etc. If the sets are tied, "1 set all" in a 3-set match, or "2 sets all" in a 5-set match, the players shall **spin again** for choice of service or side in the final set. The advantage enjoyed by player B who serves the 9th point, **providing the score is tied at 4-4,** is offset by the fact that his opponent, player A, serves 4 out of the first 6 points, namely, 1, 2, 5, and 6, and the fact that the 9th point may never be reached.

In Doubles, the same player on Team A serves points 1 and 2, his partner 5 and 6. On Team B the same player serves points 3 and 4 and his partner, points 7, 8, and 9. Each player shall serve from the side (N-S) from which he served during the preceding games in the set.

In regular VASSS play, a match may be

either 2 sets or 4 sets with the sudden death to decide the winner if sets are divided, or the regular 2 out of 3, or 3 out of 5 set match formula may be used.

HANDICAP RULES

The VASSS SINGLE POINT method is used.

Play shall proceed as if the points of the handicap had actually been played.

(a) Handicap 2 Points: Server commences serving Point 3 into Right or Forehand Court. **Service** and **Side** both change after 3 Points (2 + 3 = 5).

(b) Handicap 6 Points: Server commences serving Point 7 into the Left or Backhand Court. Service changes after 4 Points (6 + 4 = 10). Sides (N-S) are changed after 9 points (6 + 9 = 15).

The giver of the handicap shall have the **choice of Service and Side** in the opening Set, choice of Service **only** in subsequent sets. At the conclusion of the set players do not change Sides. (N-S).

TO ESTIMATE HANDICAP POINTS TO BE RECEIVED AT 30-30 IN 9-POINT TIEBREAK

1-3 Points—NO POINTS Handicap. 4-7 Points—1 Point Handicap, 8-14 Points—2 Point Handicap, 15-21 Points—3 Point Handicap, 22-30 Points—4 Point Handicap.

In the 9-Point Tiebreak handicap, points shall be considered as if already played. Examples: 1 point handicap, A shall serve point 2 into Left or Backhand court. 2 point handicap, B shall serve point 3 into Right or Forehand court.

VASSS RULES FOR SCORING ROUND ROBIN MEDAL PLAY (RRMP)

A ROUND may be any multiple of 20 (40 - 60 - 80) total points or one 31 Point set is used, the winner shall receive a 5-Point bonus for the win, plus the unplayed Points in the set (e.g.: A wins 31 - 10, his score will be 31 + 5 + 20 = 56 Points).

SERVICE AND SIDES are changed as in 31 Point. See Rules 2, 3, 4, 5.

INDIVIDUAL HANDICAPS are estimated against scratch for the number of points in a round, as decided by the tournament committee.

TOURNAMENT TEAM HANDICAP is the sum of the individual players' handicaps.

IN CASE OF A TIE, follow Tiebreak Rules.

IN FIRST-CLASS COMPETITION, ON FAST SURFACES such as grass, where the 'power serve' and 'net rushing' tactics virtually eliminate ground stroke play, IF DESIRED the balance MAY be maintained by the server serving from a line 3 feet back of the baseline, or by allowing only a single serve.

Glossary

Ace A serve that is in but is either so fast or so perfectly placed that opponent is unable to touch it.

Ad Abbreviation for "advantage."

Ad Court The correct name for the left service or backhand court. When the score is ad, the ball is always served into the ad court.

Advantage The point which follows deuce.

Advantage In If the server wins the advantage point, the score is "advantage in." If he then wins the next point, he wins the game. If he loses the next point, the score returns to deuce.

Advantage Out If the server loses the advantage point, the score becomes "advantage out." He must take the next point to bring the score back to deuce.

All The score is tied at other than deuce; i.e., 30-all or 15-all.

Alley The 4½-foot-wide area between the singles sideline and the doubles sideline on both sides of a double court.

American Twist An advance serve executed with a snap of the wrist that causes the ball to spin in flight and to bounce off high and sharply to the left when made by a right-handed server, or to the right when made by a left-handed server.

Angle Volley A stroke hit just before the ball touches the ground at such an angle that it passes the opponent out of his reach.

Approach Shot A running-in shot which a player uses to advance to the net. It must be hit deep to give him time to get there.

Australian Formation A doubles position first demonstrated in Australia in which both server and partner stand on the same side of the court, forcing the return of serve to be made down the line. The server then runs on a diagonal line to the net to take the net man's normal position.

Backcourt The 18-foot-deep area between the service line and the base line. This area is often referred to as "no-man's-land."

Backhand The stroke used to hit balls on the left side of a right-handed player and on the right side of a left-handed player. One of the basic tennis strokes.

Backspin A rotary motion applied to the ball by undercutting it so that it spins in a direction opposite to its flight pattern. This is also called underspin.

Backswing In a ground stroke, the preliminary act of taking the racket back before bringing it forward for the stroke.

Ball Boy or Girl The person, generally a junior, who retrieves balls for players in a tournament match.

Band The strip of canvas attached to the top of the tennis net.

Base Line The boundary line at the rear end of each court.

Big Game The aggressive style seen frequently in top tournament play today in which a powerhouse serve is followed immediately to net, and then followed by a hard volley which usually decides the point.

Big Server A player, usually male, with an unusually powerful serve.

Block The use of the racket to return the ball with neither a backswing nor a follow-through but rather a backstop. A ball is blocked back to an opponent most frequently in returning a powerful, fast service and is very effective when used by a woman against a big server.

Break A Serve The phrase used when a player wins a game served by his opponent.

Bullet A very hard serve.

Bye A term used in an elimination tournament for a player who is not required to play the first round. A player who receives a first-round bye is automatically qualified to play in the second round.

Canadian Doubles When only three players are available, each takes turns playing singly and with a part-ner, rotating after each set. Scores are tallied individually.

Cannonball A very hard serve, synonymous with bullet.

Carry A term applied when the racket pushes the ball rather than strokes it, or when the racket touches the ball more than once in a return.

Center Mark The 4-inch-long mark at the midpoint of the base line which defines the limits of the service position.

Center Service Line The dividing line between the two service courts.

Center Strap The 2-inch-wide piece of canvas which secures the net at the center of the court.

Change of Game A fundamental change in the strategy and style of play, often during a tournament, when the initial strategy and style prove ineffective. An old motto is: "Never change a winning game; always change a losing game."

Change of Length Shots that are made with varying lengths; i.e., a long shot followed by a short shot followed by a mid-court shot.

Change of Pace Shots that are made with varying speeds; i.e., a fast shot followed by a slow shot.

Chip A modified slice which puts underspin or backspin on the ball, usually hit in front of the body with minimum windup and follow-through.

Choke When a player tightens up and misses an easy shot, he is said to have choked the shot. The term is also applied to holding the racket too far up the handle when gripping it and may be either intentional or accidental.

Chop Synonymous with chip.

Consolation Tournament An event often held at major tournaments in which losers in early rounds compete against each other in their own tournament.

Continental Grip A compromise grip about halfway between the Eastern forehand and Eastern backhand grips often used in volleying at net to eliminate the necessity of shifting grips on the racket for forehand and backhand volleys. It is also referred to as the service grip since it is often used in serving.

Cross-Court Shot A ball which is hit diagonally from one corner of the court across the net to the other corner. The reverse of down the line.

Crossover The situation in doubles in which the net man moves across the center into the server's court as the server runs diagonally to the net to cover the court vacated by his partner. This play is sometimes referred to as a "scissors." In less advanced doubles play, where one partner plays up and the other back, the net man crosses over when his partner moves into his side of the court to return a ball. The player at the back of the court will often call "Crossover" to signal his partner to move to the other side of the court.

Deep Shot A ball which lands near or behind the base line.

Default Failure of a player to appear for; or to complete, a scheduled match.

Delivery The service.

Deuce An even score after each player or team has won three points or more in a game; i.e., 40-all etc.

Deuce Court The right service or forehand court and the court to which the ball is served at deuce.

Deuce Set A set is deuce when the score is even after ten or more games are played; i.e., when the game score is 5–5. It is then necessary to win more than the customary six games in order to win the set.

Die When a ball barely bounces at all, it is said to have died.

Dink The general term for a soft, bloopy shot which drops just over the net and generally drives an opponent to distraction.

Dip A ball that barely clears the net and then drops fast and short.

Double-Fault The failure of the server to make either his first or second serve good, which results in his losing the point.

Doubles The game of tennis played with two people on each side or team.

Down-the-Line Shot A ball which is hit roughly parallel to the sideline.

Draw The positioning of players and schedule of matches in an elimination tournament.

Drift A form of poaching in which the net man on the serving team edges or drifts toward the serving court in order to intercept a cross-court return.

Drive A forehand or backhand ground-stroke hit after the ball has bounced with a firm, full stroke, usually deep into the opponent's court.

Drive Volley A volley in which a groundstroke windup is taken. Not recommended.

Drop-Shot A ball that is hit with exaggerated underspin so that it drops immediately after clearing the net and then bounces with little or no forward motion or dies completely.

Drop Volley A volley that is hit on the fly with so much underspin that it bounces and dies like a drop-shot.

Dump A situation in which a player, in order to conserve his energy for the next set, deliberately lets up in a set and permits his opponent to win. This usually occurs midway through a losing set when additional energy would be inadequate to effect a rally, and so is conserved for the greater possibility of victory in the next set. The term is synonymous with "junk."

Duster A ball which hits the line and sprays chalk. Such a ball is good.

Eastern Grip The standard "shake hands" grip most commonly used for the forehand.

Elimination Tournament A tournament in which the field of players is reduced by half at each round, as the winner advances to the next round and the loser drops out. Most major tournaments are the elimination type.

Error Any ball which hits the net or any area outside the legal boundaries of the opponent's court, thus resulting in the loss of the point.

Face The surface or string area of the racket.

Fault Failure of the server to put his first serve in play. The server does not lose the point but is permitted a second serve without penalty.

Fifteen The first point in a game of tennis.

Finals The last and deciding match between the final two undefeated players or teams in a tournament.

Flat Serve A serve which has very little spin.

Flat Shot A ground stroke with very little spin.

Follow-Through The motion of arm and racket after the ball has been hit.

Foot-Fault An illegal step on or over the base line by a server *before* his racket makes contact with the ball. The server may legally follow through with one or both feet into the court *after* hitting the ball.

Forced Error An error that is unavoidable because of a good shot made by one's opponent.

Forcing Shot A shot which forces one's opponent either to make an outright error or an ineffectual or weak return.

Forecourt The 21-foot-deep area between the net and the service line.

Forehand The stroke used to hit balls on the right side of a right-handed player and on the left side of a left-handed player.

Forty The third point in a game of tennis.

Game The unit of scoring within a set. It takes four points to win a game and six games to win a set, except when the game score or set score is deuce, in which case play continues until one or the other side scores two consecutive points or two consecutive games to win.

Game Score The four points of a game are scored as 15, 30, 40 and *game*. A player who has scored no points has a *love* score, which is the equivalent of zero. When both players have one point each, the score is 15-all. When both players have scored two points each, the score is 30-all. The player to score the next point has the *advantage*. To win the game, he must score the next consecutive point. If he does not, the score reverts to *deuce*. To win from a deuce score, a player must score two consecutive points.

Good Shot A shot that lands on or within the proper boundary lines.

168

Grand Slam The feat of winning the Australian, British, French and U.S. singles championships all in the same year.

Grip The position of the hand on the racket when making a stroke, also the lower portion of the racket handle which is covered with leather.

Grooved Said of a player whose form and ability to stroke the ball are so consistent that they are automatic for each stroke.

Grooved Stroke A stroke which is automatic and consistent at all times.

Ground Stroke Any shot, either forehand or backhand, that is hit after the ball bounces.

Half-Court Line The center service line.

Half-Volley A stroke made by hitting the ball immediately after it has bounced when it is barely off the court. This shot is more accurately called a "pickup."

Handle The extension of the racket from the head to the gripping end.

Head The circular or oval frame and the strings of a racket.

Hitting Deep Hitting to an area close to the base line.

Hitting Short Hitting near or within the service line.

Hold Serve When a player wins the games he serves.

In Play A ball is "in play" from the moment at which it is served until the point is decided.

Junk A slang term used for any ball which is soft or miss-hit.

Keeping Him Honest Another slang term used when a ball is hit to a spot just vacated by a poaching net man. It is comparable to catching a player off base in baseball.

Kill Usually a smash hit overhead before the ball bounces, and out of reach of the opponent.

Ladder A competitive system, generally less formal than official tournament play, in which players in a club or group are ranked according to ability and their names are listed on a chart set up like the rungs on a ladder. Each player may challenge either the player ranked immediately above him or ranked two places above him, and he may be challenged by the two players ranked immediately below him. If he wins the match with a higher ranked player, he moves ahead on the ladder into that player's position. If he loses to a higher ranked player, his position remains the same, but if he loses to a challenger, he then forfeits his position on the ladder to the winner and drops back into the challenger's former position. Most ladders are operative for an entire season or year, at the end of which the player who winds up on top is the winner.

Let Any ball that is played over without penalty either because of outside interference or other extenuating circumstances. The most common let ball is one which strikes the net in service and then falls into the proper service court.

Linesman An official who is assigned to determining whether a ball lands within the proper area of the court. In major tournaments, separate linesmen are often assigned to each boundary.

Lob Any ball that is hit high into the air, usually over the head of an opponent. Defensive lobs are usually hit in order to permit the player to get back in position after having been pulled wide of the court.

Offensive lobs are usually hit to win outright points when an opponent is up at net and unable to reach a high base-line lob.

Long A ball which falls beyond the base line in play, or beyond the service line when served.

Love Zero, or no score.

Match Competition between two players or two teams consisting of a specified number of games or sets.

Match Point The last point needed to win a match.

Mixed Doubles Play in which opposing teams consist of a man and a woman, often resulting in mixed emotions.

Mix Up Changing the pace of play and varying shots.

Net The netting placed across the middle of the court.

Net Ball Any shot after the serve that hits the net but remains in play.

Net Cord The cord which runs along the top of the net. Also a shot which hits the net cord and topples over into the opposite court, scoring a point.

Net Game A game that is played predominantly at net rather than from the back court.

Net Man The player in doubles who plays at the net while his partner serves. Also known as the net player.

No-Man's-Land The area between the base line and the service line; any player caught there is almost certainly headed for disaster.

On Serve An expression used to describe a match in which no service break has occurred; i.e., in which each player has won the games he has served.

One-Up, One-Back A tandem formation in doubles in which one partner plays at net and one plays back. Although rarely seen in championship-level tennis, this is a favorite of the novice. It is also useful when one player is considerably more advanced than his partner.

Open Racket Face When the strings of the racket are parallel or almost parallel to the ground rather than perpendicular to it.

Open Tennis Tournaments in which both amateurs and professionals compete together.

Overhead A shot made from a high position with a hard overhead stroke which sends the ball down sharply into the opponent's courts. This shot is often called a smash or kill shot.

Overhead Smash Same as above except the shot is usually hit so hard that it is impossible for the opponent to get near it or return it.

Pace A ball that is both fast and well hit is said to have pace.

Passing Shot A ball that the net player is unable to reach on either side.

Pat Ball A soft service.

Permanent Fixtures Any objects situated around the court, including the umpire, linesmen, spectators in stands or on preset chairs, the stands, chairs, net, posts, back and sidestops, fences.

Placement An outright winning shot that is hit out of an opponent's reach.

Poach The situation in which the net man moves into his partner's normal territory in order to hit or intercept a shot. If he succeeds, he is a hero; if he fails, his face deserves to be red.

Point The basic or smallest unit of the score. Four points win a game.

Post The wooden or metal upright supporting the net.

Press To force or attack the opponent. Also the wooden frame that is fitted over a wood racket to prevent it from warping.

Putaway An outright winning shot.

Quarter-Finals The round in an elimination tournament in which the field of players is reduced from eight to four.

Racket The sporting implement used to hit the ball; may be made of wood, metal, fiberglass or a combination of these materials. Do not attempt to play the game without one.

Rally In pregame practice, the exchange of balls across the net to warm up the players. In actual play, the exchange of balls between the service and the winning point when the ball passes back and forth across the net several times.

Reading One's Opponent The ability to anticipate accurately the moves of one's opponent before he makes them by observing small clues from his body position, stance, prelude to stroke. An advantageous talent.

Receiver The player who receives the serve.

Referee The official in charge of a tournament who may or may not be the umpire.

Retrieve To return a difficult shot.

Retriever A player who consistently runs down and returns difficult shots.

Reverse Backhand A shot hit backwards over the net by a player facing in the other direction.

Reverse Formation Another term for the Australian formation.

Reverse Twist A rarely used service in which the racket is moved across the ball in a leftward direction.

Round-Robin A tournament in which each entrant plays every other entrant on a rotating basis until every entrant or team of entrants has played every other an equal number of times. High score wins.

Round of Sixteen The round preceding the quarter-finals in an elimination tournament in which the field is reduced from sixteen players to eight.

Running-In Shot A stroke made and followed to the net.

Rushing the Net To advance to the net in offensive play.

Scissors The crossover technique used in doubles.

Seeding The system by which the best players in an elimination tournament are separated from each other in the initial draw to prevent their coming up against each other in the early stages of the competition.

Semifinals The round in an elimination tournament in which the field of players is reduced from four to two.

Serve To put the ball into play.

Server The player who puts the ball into play.

Service Synonym for serve.

Service Break A game in which the server or the serving team loses.

Service Court The area in which the ball must land for it to be legally in play. There are two service courts, a left and a right, each 21 feet deep and 13½ feet wide. The same service courts are used in singles and doubles.

Service Line The rear boundary of the service courts.

Set The unit of scoring which follows game scoring. Six winning games are required to win a set, unless one's opponent has won five games, in which case the set must be won by two games more than one's opponent.

Set Point The last point needed to win a set.

Set Score The number of games required to win a set which is expressed by giving the winner's score first, followed by the loser's score; i.e., 6–1, 6–2, 7–5, 8–6, etc.

Setup A shot that is made in such a manner that it can be put away for an outright winner. An easy mark.

Side-by-Side Formation The most popularly used alignment of partners in doubles wherein both players either play back or play net together.

Sidelines The left and right boundaries of either the singles or doubles court.

Side Service Line The left and right boundaries of the service courts which in singles are also the sidelines.

Sidespin The spin produced by brushing the racket forward and toward the body as it strokes the ball.

Singles The game of tennis involving one person on either side of the net.

Sitter A shot that seems to hang momentarily in the air, inviting a putaway.

Slice A stroke in which the racket is drawn sharply down across the ball with exaggerated wrist action to give it heavy sidespin.

Slice Serve A serve in which the racket comes across the ball sideways and forward at the same time, putting sidespin on the serve.

Spin The rotating motion of the ball in any direction.

Stop Volley A drop volley.

Stroke The motion of striking the ball with the racket.

Sweet Spot The section of the strings in the very center of the racket head. When the ball is stroked off this point, it carries maximum pace and control.

Take the Net When a player advances to the net to volley.

Tandem Formation Another name for the Australian formation.

Tape A canvas band that covers the net cord at the top of the net.

Thirty The second point of a game.

Three-Bounce Rule A modification of the official rules designed to encourage longer rallies. It prohibits both players from advancing to the net until the ball has bounced three times.. Rare in tournament play.

Throat The part of the racket between the handle and the head.

Top Spin A rotary motion of the ball caused by stroking up and over it. Also known as overspin. The ball usually spins forward or bounces high after hitting the court.

Touch Artist A player with a broad command of spins and delicate shots.

Touch Shot Any shot which requires extreme delicacy and control, such as a drop-shot or lob volley.

Toss The act of spinning or throwing up the racket for choice of service court before a match. In serving, the act of throwing up the ball by the server.

Tournament Any official competition.

Twist A serve hit with a combination of sidespin and top spin.

Umpire The top-ranking on-court official in a particular match who may or may not also be the off-court referee of the tournament. The decision of the umpire overrules that of a linesman.

Underspin A backward rotation of the

ball in opposition to its flight path. Also called backspin.

USLTA The United State Lawn Tennis Association; the major governing body of amateur tennis in the U.S.

VASSS Van Alen Simplified Scoring System, developed by the legendary James Van Alen in an attempt to popularize tennis for the "common man" by adapting a 21-point scoring system similar to that used in table tennis. Although the system has been tried widely in the past two decades, it has not replaced conventional scoring.

Volley Any stroke made by hitting the ball before it touches or bounces on the ground.

Western Grip An outmoded and somewhat awkward method of holding the racket.

Wide A ground stroke or service that lands outside the side boundaries.

Wide-Breaking Slice A service or ground stroke that pulls the receiver outside or wide of the side boundary in order to return it, if he can.

Wood Shot A shot hit off the frame or handle of the racket instead of on the strings. Players with metal rackets do the same thing occasionally but call their affliction a "metal shot." Neither is recommended.

Wrong Foot A ball that is hit behind an opponent after he has already begun moving in the other direction. It is generally impossible to return. Basically the same as "to catch an opponent leaning."

Zilch The expression used for any shot that goes into the net, out of bounds or onto another court.

Index

Page numbers in boldface refer to illustrations

Adjustment foot, 51, 53, 89
Almonte, Ramón "Chollo," 16, 22, 24, 28
Anchor foot, **50**, 51, **52**, **65**, 67, **73**, 74, **82**, **83**, 84
Anticipation, 128–129
Ashe, Arthur, 119

Backboard, 18–19, 23, 105, 108
Backhand balance, 51, **52**, 53
Backhand drive, 19, **35**, 51, 63, 64, 79–91, 124, **128**
    exercises, 86–87
    two–handed, 89–90
Backhand grip, 16, 57, **57**, **58**, 59, 60
    Eastern, **58**, 59, 60, 61, 62
Backhand volley, 63, 97, 98, 99, **101**, 102, **102**, **103**, 105, **106**
Backswing, 124
    backhand drive, 80, **81**, 84, **84**, **86**, 87, **90**
    forehand drive, 65, **65**, **68**, **69**, 70, 73
    lob, 95
    ovehead smash, 121
    serve, 112, 113, 118
Balance, 15, 49–53, 79, 80
    backhand, 51, **52**, 53
    forehand, 49, **50**, 51
Ball Boy machine, 39–41
Balls, tennis, 138–139
Balls out, calling, 142–143, 145
Bartkowicz, Peaches, 18
Budge, Don, 56–57

Calls
    balls out, 142–143
    score, 142
Cannonball, 124
Cheating, 145
Clothing, 137
Concentration, 128, 129–131, 135
Continental grip, 60, **60**, 61, 62
Conversation on court, avoidance of, 145–146
Court, tennis, diagram and dimensions of, **150**, **161**
Courtesy, 23, 136–148
Courtsmanship, 136–148
Cross-court drive, 127

Doubles game rules, 160–161

Drives. *See* Backhand drive;
    Cross-court drive;
    Forehand drive
Drop-shot, 63, 92, 93
Drysdale, Cliff, 89

Eastern backhand grip, **58**, 59, 60, 61, 62
Eastern forehand grip, 53, 55, **55**, **56**, 56–57, 59, 60, 62, 110, **110**, 117
Elbow, tennis, 25–26
Errors, 127, 135, 144
    calling, 145
Etiquette, 136–148
Evert, Chris, 31, 89
Exercises
    backhand drive, 80–87
    forehand drive, 64–70
    preliminary, 48–51, 64–65
    racket-tossing, 115
    serving, 109–115
    volleying, 105

Fatigue, fighting, 135
Follow through, 16, 18, **54**, **66**, **67**, 67, 69, 70, 73, 74, 77, 79, **83**, 84, **85**, 89, **91**, 95, 124
Foot-faulting, 113–114, 144
Footwork, 15, 32, 70, 113–114, 128, **128**, 131–132, **133**, **134**, 135
Forehand balance, 49, **50**, 51
Forehand drive, 19, 53, 63, 64–79, 124, **133**
    exercises, 64–70
Forehand grip, 16
    Eastern, 53, 55, **55**, **56**, 56–57, 59, 60, 62, 110, **110**, 117
Forehand volley, 63, 97, 98, 99, **100**, 105
Fundamentals of tennis, 15, 48–49, 79, 127, 136

Glossary, 165–173
Grip, 15, 49, 53–62
    backhand, 16, 57, **57**, **58**, 59, 60
        Eastern, **58**, 59, 60, 61, 62
    Continental, 60, **60**, 61, 62
    forehand, 16
        Eastern 53, 55, **55**, **56**, 56–57, 59, 60, 62, 110, **110**, 117
    service, 62
    Western, 60, **61**, 61–62

Index

Ground strokes, 63, 64, 98
Group lessons, 46

Half-volley, 63, 92–93, **93,** 131
Handicap rules, 164
Hartman, Ezra, 34–35, **35,** 36, 41, 42, 43, 131
Hip ball, 106, **106**
Honesty, 144–145
Hopman, Harry, 107
Hoxie, Jean, 18
Humor, tennis and, 136

Improvising, **133, 134,** 135

King, Billie Jean, 107–108

Ladies' tennis, 21–22, 36–38
Let ball, 142–143
Lob, 63, 92, 93–96, 135
   cross-court, 95
   defensive, 94
   offensive, 94
   outrageous, 94–95

Moody Trainer, 19, 20, 23, 32

Overconfidence, 135
Overhead serve, 63
Overhead smash, 63, 121, **122,** 123, **123**

Pasarell, Charles, 12
Perry, Fred, 61
Pivoting, 16, **50,** 51, 53, 57, 65, 67, 79, **85,**
   90, 112, 114, 121, **133**
Placement, 40, 124, 127
Position, body, 15

Racket-tossing exercise, 115
Rackets, 14, 16, 26, 53, 78
Reaction time, 39, 125
Ready position, 57, 59, **59,** 60, 69, 80, 84, 94,
   98, 124–125, 126
Return of serve, 124–126
Rhythm, 18, 117, 121
Riggs, Bobby, 12
Rules
   doubles game, 160–161

handicap, 164
singles game, 149–160

Score, calling the, 142
Segura, Pancho, 89
Serve, 18, 63, 64, 107–120, 121
   American Twist, 112
   hippy, **110**
   overhead, 63
   return of, 124–126
   shot-put, **112**
Service grip, 62
Singles game rules, 149–160
Steadiness, 127.
Strategy, 15, 49, 127–135
Strike zone, 16, 41, 73, **73,** 74, **74,** 75, 84, 89
Strokes, 15, 16, 17, 18, 19, 49, 53, 63, 68
   ground, 63, 64, 98
   net, 97
   See also names of strokes

Terms, glossary of, 164–172
Tilden, Bill, 123, 126
Timing, 18, 19, 78, 79, 93, 94, 95, 98, 116,
   117, 121, 142
Toss, service, 116–117, **117,** 118, 121

Umpires, 142

Van der Meer, Dennis, 74
Van Horn, Welby, 12–29, 31, 32, 35, 37, 40,
   45–47, 49, 51, 74, 127, 135, 136
Volleying, 19, 37, 40, 61, 97–106
   exercises, 105
Volleys, 63
   backhand, 63, 97, 98, 99, **101, 102,** 102,
      103, 105, **106**
   drop, 63, 97
   forehand, 63, 97, 98, 99, **100,** 105
   lob, 63, 97
   low, **104,** 104–105

Warming up, 137–138
Western grip, 60, **61,** 61–62
Windmill player, 75–76, 118